MINISTRY
IN HARD TIMES

MINISTRY
IN HARD TIMES

BILL EASUM
BILL TENNY-BRITTIAN

ABINGDON PRESS / Nashville

MINISTRY IN HARD TIMES

Copyright © 2010 by Abingdon Press

All rights reserved.

This book is printed on acid-free paper.

Library of Congress Cataloging-in-Publication Data

Easum, William M., 1939-
  Ministry in hard times / Bill Easum, Bill Tenny-Brittian.
    p. cm.
  ISBN 978-1-4267-0842-8 (binding: trade pbk., adhesive : alk. paper)
  1. Church finance. 2. Financial crises. 3. Pastoral theology. I. Tenny-Brittian, William.
II. Title.
  BV770.E28 2010
  254'.8090511—dc22

2009041382

Scripture quotations, unless otherwise noted, are taken from the New Revised Standard Version of the Bible, copyright 1989, Division of Christian Education of the National Council of the Churches of Christ in the United States of America. Used by permission. All rights reserved.

Scripture quotations noted NASB are taken from the *New American Standard Bible®*, Copyright © 1960, 1962, 1963, 1968, 1971, 1972, 1973, 1975, 1977, 1995 by The Lockman Foundation. Used by permission. (www.Lockman.org)

Scripture quotations noted NIV are taken from the Holy Bible, NEW INTERNATIONAL VERSION®. Copyright © 1973, 1978, 1984 by International Bible Society. All rights reserved throughout the world. Used by permission of International Bible Society.

10 11 12 13 14 15 16 17 18 19—10 9 8 7 6 5 4 3 2 1

MANUFACTURED IN THE UNITED STATES OF AMERICA

CONTENTS

A COMMENT ON THE TIMES

Taking It on the Chin

These are very bad times for the vast majority of people in the world. As of this writing, we are looking to be in one of the worst years since the Great Depression. Savings and pensions were cut in half. Major banks and businesses failed. More than one and a half million jobs have been lost, with no end in sight. Trillions of dollars in government bailouts have been doled out. And there's an overall lack of confidence in governments around the world. Everyone is experiencing economic shock.

An economic crisis is no time to tweak your church budget. It is not the time to slash and burn it indiscriminately across the board, nor even to hunker down in the bunker and wait things out. Now is the time to exercise wisdom and to act strategically. In fact, it's a great time to be the church. People need us to live out our mission as radically as we can possibly imagine.

This book will help you make wise decisions about how to weather the economic storm and emerge on the other side of it a much stronger congregation. It's a simple book filled with wise advice.

Bill Easum
Bill Tenny-Brittian

ONE

LIVING IN A
WILDCARD WORLD

E ven if you haven't been paying attention, you must be painfully aware that we're living in difficult times. We've had difficult times before, but these times are significantly different. We're living in a time when the world is being whipsawed by a number of potential wildcards, any one of which is enough to disrupt the fabric of society.

Wildcards are major events that come out of nowhere, totally unforeseen by the common person, and change everything. As a result, virtually nothing is the same as it used to be; it's a whole new world.

Most of our (BE: Bill Easum; and BTB: Bill Tenny-Brittian) lives have been lived in a world of probabilities. Probability is the likelihood or chance that something will happen. Probability theory is used in statistics, mathematics, science, and philosophy to draw conclusions about the likelihood of potential events. For most of our lives, it was easy to survey the landscape and have a fair idea of the probability of where the future was heading. The only really serious wildcard was nuclear war—until recently.

Today's world is filled with more wildcards than probabilities. If we were to list all the wildcards, this book would be too long. So let us mention a few of them in the order of their potential negative impact.

1

Terrorism
Global warming
Nuclear war
U.S. decline as a world power
Rise of China and Iran
Pakistan
Volatile world stock markets
Oil prices

These wildcards haven't been played yet. They are just potential wildcards. However, two wildcards not on the above list have been dealt and they are changing the balance of life throughout the world, making for hard times for the vast majority of people.

THE CULTURAL WILDCARD

We have the dubious privilege of living in a time of two gut-wrenching wildcards. The first wildcard began sometime around the middle of the twentieth century and is what many historians describe as a "five-hundred-year hinge of history." In my book *Dancing with Dinosaurs* I called it a "crack in history."[1] Every five hundred years or so the world goes crazy and empties itself of all its guts. We like the metaphor Phyllis Tickle uses in her book *The Great Emergence*—every once in a while the church cleans out its attic and holds a giant rummage sale.[2]

The last such major cultural upheaval was the Protestant Reformation five hundred years ago. Just as the Reformation and the printing press changed the world forever, so the midpoint to the end of the twentieth century changed the world forever again.

This cultural upheaval is wreaking havoc in most organizations, turning them upside down. Only the strongest and most nimble organizations are surviving this wildcard. Just look at the Fortune 500 companies. Very few of the companies on the list in 1980 are still among the top 500.

Our churches haven't escaped the ravages of this cultural upheaval either. Just about everything traditional Christianity was based upon since the Protestant Reformation has been under siege for the past fifty years, and in the last ten years the sacking of traditional Christianity has become almost complete. All one has to do is take stock of the shape of the vast majority of churches more than thirty years old and it is clear that most of established Christianity is in shambles.

Recently we have been using two new metaphors to help explain what has happened as a result of this cultural upheaval. We characterize the world prior to the cultural upheaval as the "National Park world" and the new world emerging as a result of the revolution as the "jungle."

Let your imagination run wild as we briefly unpack these two metaphors.

THE NATIONAL PARK WORLD

Most people have been to at least one national park at least once in their lifetime. Driving through a national park, one can't help but notice how everything is neatly laid out in a highly controlled environment. You don't need a compass. There is never any doubt you are on the road that will take you where you want to go. It's tough to get lost in a national park.

National parks are extremely safe if you follow the rules. They are full of "do this" and "don't do this" rules you are supposed to follow. National parks even warn you about dangerous animals, making the national park a safe place even when you are around things that might harm you. You are warned when you are about to enter an area where you shouldn't go or get out of your car or take a hiking trail that might be too steep for you. Since national parks are so safe, it is OK to travel them alone, even at night, so long as you obey the rules.

National parks are predictable and slow to change. You can go to a national park year after year and never see much change, and what change you do see is slow and incremental.

3

Your taxes pay for the national park, so you are entitled to experience all of its wonders and delights. You may even feel a sense of partial ownership of the park.

You have no problem seeing the horizon in a national park. You can always see where you are going—and when you can't, you can follow the signs. There's no need for a compass or GPS in a national park.

Christianity is royalty in the national park. People respect the Christian church and want one in their neighborhood, so much so that developers set land aside for them.

People take on the appearance of being happy and content in the national park. Even when some difficulty raises its head and threatens to ruin one's stay, people in the national park put their best foot forward, keep their chins up, and keep a stiff upper lip.

In the national park world, men were the dominant figures. The wife mostly worked in the home, the family was nuclear, the world was described as a collection of nation-states, divorce was frowned upon, children were taught the Bible, Grandma was nearby, the nation was not as mobile, Scripture and the church were the basic authority, abortion was illegal, Lawrence Welk was in, and homosexuality was a sin. Ozzy and Harriet were the role models for life.

Most established church people are still very much at home in the national park world. Like an ostrich burying its head in the sand, many church leaders refuse to accept the fact that the national park world is swiftly disappearing—who are we kidding? That world is almost gone.

THE JUNGLE

One of my (BE) favorite places in the world is a little place called Tropic Star Lodge, located at the end of the Darien jungle on the border of Panama and Colombia. The lodge is cut off from the world by two hundred miles of some of the densest rain forest in the world. I go there to fish, not to visit the jungle. But on one trip the allure of the dense jungle drew me in—and was it an eye-opener. I had never been in such a foreboding place in all my life. Nothing was familiar and everything shouted out a warning. My experience that day gave me a hint of what the emerging world was going to look like in full bloom.

The jungle is quite different from the national park.

In the jungle, nothing is neatly laid out and controlled, making it a really messy place. Nothing is where you would expect it to be and you have very little control over the environment. In a jungle world, intuition is one of the most needed talents of a leader, surpassing even passion. At best, messy and uncontrollable environments confuse most established church people; at worst, these environments shut them down when they are faced with making strategic decisions.

Predators are everywhere in the jungle and there aren't any hard and fast rules to follow, making it an extremely unsafe environment. The rules of the national park no longer apply. No signs warn about the various predators. It's almost as if the jungle dares you to test its will. Many established church people are too naïve to recognize the reality of the jungle and the heresies that leap out from every corner. The jungle does away with all rules except one—the survival of the fittest.

Nothing is predictable in the jungle. It changes dramatically from day to day. Trails can be covered overnight with all manner of vegetation; all markers can vanish, leaving a traveler lost without an experienced guide. Established church people find it impossible to move fast enough to stay up with the changes, much less get ahead of them.

You are on your own for shelter in the jungle, making it an uncomfortable place to spend time. One has to keep moving all the time—there's little time to sit and think. Established church people find no comfort or solace without their buildings, and that confuses them terribly.

You're not entitled to be in the jungle. It doesn't belong to us, and we have to earn our right to exist in the jungle. It's as if the jungle delights in making us feel like aliens in a strange world. Established church people are miserable when confronted with the fact that the world no longer owes them a living and their pastor isn't their spiritual babysitter.

No one ventures into the jungle alone because it is so unsafe and complex. You need a team to navigate it—someone to watch your back, both sides, and the front, just to survive, much less get to your destination. Established church people find it hard to transition from committees to autonomous team-based ministries.

In the jungle, when you look up there is no horizon. The sun rarely shines through the jungle canopy. The trees are so thick at the top they block the sun, making the jungle seem creepy, dark, and damp. The canopy is so dense a GPS won't work in many parts of the jungle, so when travelers come to a clearing they quickly enter the clearing and take a GPS reading to confirm their heading. Then they quickly return to the dense jungle because they know they are more vulnerable in a clearing than in the jungle itself. In such an environment one needs a very clear sense of direction. Jesus is the only reliable compass in the jungle.

As far as the jungle is concerned, Christianity lacks meaning or significance. Gone are the days when society gave credence and special favor to Christianity. Now it's just the opposite—the jungle dislikes Christianity because the jungle doesn't recognize it as legitimate. Fewer people come to the church on their own now. Established church people are shocked to learn that society talks about the day when Christianity will be taxed like any other business.

Most people and organizations in the jungle are basically broken. The jungle has a way of tearing families apart and enabling people to become addicted to one thing or another. Ozzie and Harriet have been replaced by Ozzy Osborne as a model.

Organizations that were once vital no longer yield the same results. When someone comes into a church from the jungle, they have little understanding of Christianity. What they are looking for is a safe place to find themselves or to heal. Established church people still think all they have to do is repeat some predetermined formula, dogma, or doctrine and all will be well with the world.

In the jungle the nuclear family is dead; divorce is easy; abortion is legal; homosexual marriage is gaining acceptance; the wife is just as likely as the husband to be the major bread-winner; children grow up not knowing the Bible or Christian values; Grandma doesn't live next door but many miles away; no one knows who lives next door; and Scripture and the church are no longer the basic authority.

No wonder the last fifty years have been so debilitating for most established churches. They're living in a strange land try-ing to play by rules that no longer exist and they are being eaten alive.

> How the church responds to this crisis could determine much of what happens to North American Christianity for decades to come.

THE FINANCIAL WILDCARD

As if the cultural upheaval wasn't enough to do most estab-lished churches in, the worldwide disaster has left most peo-ple in the West much poorer than a year ago. We've witnessed the collapse of stock markets around the world. Savings and pensions have been cut in half. Jobs have been lost. Banks and major financial institutions have failed. And there's a lack of confidence in governments and financial institutions around the world. Everyone seems to be waiting for the next shoe to drop or the next job to be lost.

Churches are not exempt from this downturn.[3] All across the United States, church leaders seem to be hunkering down and turning their focus inward. Much of the world is gripped by fear and retreating into a bunker mentality.

NOW'S NOT THE TIME TO PANIC

I (BE) remember the first time it dawned on me in early 2008 that my life's savings were in dire jeopardy. For a couple of weeks I couldn't do anything. I found myself waking up in the middle of the night in a cold sweat. I couldn't even bring myself to look at my portfolio because I knew what was happening—it was gradually vanishing, almost daily.

What you have to understand is that as of this writing I stand on the threshold of my seventieth birthday. I won't have time to rebuild what my family has lost the past twelve months. So this loss for us, like many people our age, is catastrophic. And the thought of my wife and me winding up broke in some state-supported rest home after more than fifty years of ministry was almost more than I could bear.

Finally God intervened and said three things to me: "Sell." "Be calm." "Write a book so others won't panic and harm the mission."

All across the United States, people just like me are shell-shocked from losing a large portion of their life savings. Others have lost their jobs or are afraid of losing them. How the church responds to this crisis could determine much of what happens to North American Christianity for decades to come.

Panicking won't help. So don't do it! I (BTB) remember learning in the Dale Carnegie Course, many years ago, that there's no sense in worrying about things we cannot change—and if there's something we *can* change, then there's no sense in worrying about it if we'll do what we need to do.

We want to encourage you not to panic and freeze or slash the budget or go into a survival mode. It doesn't do any good to be recklessly reactive just because times are tough. Nor are hard times the time for a hunker-in-the-bunker mentality. Instead, now is the time to be more strategic and aggressive than ever before.

THE PURPOSE OF THIS BOOK

The purpose of this book is to give you calm, wise counsel on how to be proactive so you can remain strong until things turn around and emerge stronger on the other side of these cultural and financial wildcards. We don't promise the jungle will go away, but you can learn to live and function in it.

This book is neither long nor difficult to follow. We will strive to give you the best advice for doing ministry in hard times in as few words as possible. However, we won't pull any punches. What you are about to read is not always going to be easy to stomach. But it is the truth and it will help guide you through the jungle. Thus this book is designed to:

- Help churches make strategic decisions about how to spend their time, energy, and money during hard times;
- Help church people cope with the spiritual and psychological conditions Christians face in hard times;
- Help churches remain strong and emerge stronger on the other side of hard times.

SUGGESTED READING

Dancing with Dinosaurs, by Bill Easum. Abingdon Press (1993), 132 pp.

Extraordinary Leaders in Extraordinary Times, ed. by H. Stanley Wood. Eerdmans Press (2006), 188 pp.

Surfing the Edge of Chaos, by Richard T. Pascale, Mark Milleman, and Linda Gioja. Three Rivers Press (2001), 336 pp.

Notes

1. William Easum. *Dancing with Dinosaurs* (Nashville: Abingdon Press, 1993).

2. Phyllis Tickle. *The Great Emergence* (Grand Rapids: Baker Books, 2008), 17–19.

3. In a new GuideStar survey, over one-third of the charities surveyed raised less money in the first nine months of 2008 than they did in the same period the previous year. Half of the charities that rely heavily on end-of-year gifts expect donations to be less robust for the rest of the year. This survey was taken before the most recent market drops. http://www.guidestar.org/news/features/2008_survey.pdf

TWO

STRATEGIC DREAMING TRUMPS HARD TIMES

Hard times can either bring great opportunities for service and growth or they can bring great hardships to churches and their leaders. Only one thing determines the difference—how church leaders react to the hard times.

If hard times are seen as an opportunity to make strategic changes designed to counteract the situation, the congregation can come through the hard times a much stronger church. If, however, the hard times are seen as a serious threat to the survival of the congregation, prompting church leaders to hunker down with a slash-and-burn mentality, the odds are the congregation will come through the hard times a much weaker church. Outlook and attitude can make all the difference.

Sure, there are lots of negatives to hard times. The list is long. But there are also huge positives in hard times:

- Hard times cause Christians to refocus on what matters most to them in life.
- Hard times tend to drive out irrelevant and obsolete ministries and practices.
- Hard times cause strategic leaders to return to the basics.
- Hard times often result in unchurched people showing up in worship.

- Hard times require that special attention be paid to spiritual formation.

To explain how this works, let me (BE) share a true story with you.

In the mid-80s all of Texas underwent an oil bust. Just about everyone in the state was seriously affected by the downturn in the oil business. I estimated that one-quarter of our church entered bankruptcy and among that group were our best givers. When the dust settled, we estimated that over the next twelve months we would wind up approximately $150,000 short on an $800,000 budget. We faced a serious challenge.

Our board wanted to slash the budget by the same amount. That meant letting some key staff people go and cancelling some major ministries. I was determined that neither of these things would happen under my watch.

So our staff got together and did what I call "Strategic Dreaming." Strategic dreaming is simply asking, "What can we do to change the reality of the situation?" In this specific instance the question was "What can we do to come through these hard times stronger than we entered them without cutting the budget or letting staff go?" "How can we turn these hard times into a positive for our church?"

We knew business as usual wouldn't allow us to come through the hard times unscathed, much less stronger. So the staff laid down some strategic ground rules as to how we would function:

- We would do whatever it took to continue growing and doing effective ministry during the hard times.
- We would cut every nonessential item from the budget.
- No one in pastoral/program ministry would lose his or her job, but he or she might be asked to take a pay cut.
- Nothing would ever be mentioned from the pulpit about feeling bad about the hard times. Instead, all sermons would be positive.

With these four ground rules, we did our strategic dreaming. For several weeks the staff met, prayed, and dreamed. During that time period, two things rose to the surface. To have a chance to get through the hard times, we had to do the following:

- The leaders had to be in constant prayer to stay spiritually and psychologically strong for the church.
- The people making the financial decisions had to be limited to one or two people and both of them needed to be on staff. (Our staff was capable of doing this. If yours isn't capable of making these decisions, look for one or two laypeople who don't receive a weekly or monthly paycheck but who get paid periodically throughout the year based on how they perform.) Why the limit of one or two people? Because effective strategic decisions are seldom made by a committee. The more people sitting in the room, the less strategic budget-cutting and redirecting of funds will happen. All one has to do is take a look at how Congress addresses hard times. No matter what kind of bill comes out of Congress, it is always full of pork. The government can print money; the church can't.

The above two items may not appear like much, but consider that when we made this decision our denomination required a church our size to have around three hundred and sixty people on the board and committees. Can you imagine getting that many people to agree on a strategic decision, much less do strategic dreaming? Impossible.

So we approached the board with this proposal—shut down the board and all committees, cut all nonessential ministries, and permit the staff to make all of the decisions over the next eighteen months, and the staff would guarantee the deficit. All key, full-time pastoral/program staff members were united in this proposal.

The board accepted the proposal, and in the next week we went from nearly three hundred and sixty people making decisions and running ministries to eleven people making all the decisions, with two people having the final say in how the money was spent.

And guess what? We ended the eighteen months with more people in worship, more money in the bank, and all the pastoral/program staff intact. When the church was asked whether it wanted to return to the old form of doing ministry and organization, it declined. We took a serious negative and turned it into a positive.

Because we saw the hard times as a glass half full we were able to do away with one of the most debilitating aspects of modernity—a big bureaucracy. No church needs that many people making decisions, not if it wants to be healthy. Since then we've learned that Willow Creek has six people on its board; Bay Area Fellowship in Corpus Christi has three; and Fellowship in Dallas has three. And most dying churches with two hundred people in worship have an average of thirty or more on their board. The solution isn't rocket science. It's strategic dreaming.

A FEW RULES FOR HARD TIMES

Now, we're not comparing the hard times of the mid-80s with what we are experiencing now. No way. What we are experiencing now is far worse. It is worldwide. But we did learn a few rules about doing ministry in hard times that will serve the church well in these much harder times.

- Don't go into debt unless you absolutely have to. In hard times debt is the one thing you don't want.
- Return to the basics. No matter what you do best or how you redirect money within the budget, if the church doesn't function as a church, nothing really matters. More on this in chapter 3.
- Focus on what you do best. This will differ from church to church, but it must not be something like church bazaars. Hopefully it will be one of the items to increase in the Hard Times Budget. More on this in chapter 4.

- Cut the budget strategically rather than across the board. Cutting across the board always results in a crippled organization. More on this in chapter 5.
- Cut office personnel to the bare bones. Support personnel have a way over the years of taking up more and more space whether it's needed or not. This area of ministry is always vulnerable in hard times. More on this in chapter 5.
- Don't spend anything you don't think will result in more people in worship. Worship is your bread and butter, so it should receive the lion's share of your time, energy, and money. More on this in chapter 7.
- Strengthen your children's ministry in any way you can afford. Even in the most difficult of times, parents are as concerned about their children's well-being as they are their financial situation. More on this in chapter 7.
- Focus on evangelism and market, market, market in any way you can afford. In hard times it is imperative that you do whatever you can to tell your story and invite people. More on this in chapter 8.
- Focus more attention on adult spiritual formation. Of course, small groups are one of the key ways to develop spiritually mature leaders. Growing spiritual giants who can lead from a biblical perspective is a key to making it through good times, much less bad times. More on this in chapter 10.
- Limit the people making the financial decisions to one or two paid staff people. We've already discussed the wisdom of this rule. A different type of leadership is required in hard times. We will unpack this in chapter 11.

SO WHAT IS STRATEGIC DREAMING, ANYWAY?

Strategic dreaming is much different from strategic planning. Historically, strategic planning results in a five-year plan that is updated and expanded every fourth year so there is always a five-year plan in the works. In a wildcard world like ours today, nothing remains in place for five years, nor does it work itself out quite so neatly.

The fact is, we don't have time in a warp-speed world to do strategic planning. Moreover, there's not enough reliable information on hand about the emerging jungle culture and the economic mess we're in to rely on strategic plans. On the other hand, we must chart a course for our journey to navigate our way through these hard times. But here's the catch—by necessity this chart will have to be drawn on the fly. That's where strategic dreaming and strategic planning go their separate ways.

Strategic plans are drawn before one begins the journey, based on the information at hand. Once a plan is complete, one of two things usually happens. Either people follow the plan faithfully, even when it's not working, because they've invested so much in creating it that they can't bear to discard it, or the plan is left on a shelf to gather dust.

On the other hand, anyone who has ever charted and navigated a course knows that course corrections take up more than 99 percent of the navigator's time. Likewise, a strategic dreaming map gets drawn while the journey is underway. It's never set in concrete like most strategic plans; it's always in flux.

The Exodus experience is an excellent biblical example of strategic dreaming. While taking the people from Egypt to Canaan, Moses had some idea of the heading, but he had no concrete plans for getting from Egypt to Canaan. He just knew anything was better than making mud bricks in slavery. So he started out on the journey. Strategic dreaming is starting out on the journey with a general idea of where you want to go, yet being flexible enough to take detours, reroute, or even start over again if that's what it takes to reach the destination. The destination is more important than the plan itself.

The reason so many church leaders have problems understanding and accepting this difference is that most of our churches are still firmly in the grasp of the national park, which includes management by objective, strategic planning, rationality, linear direction, cost-benefit analysis, quality control, and continual improvement. In the jungle, however, organizations find themselves gradually moving in directions they never intended or planned. And if something works, in retrospect they label it a deliberate strategy or a strategic plan. In other words, a lot of strategic planning isn't very strategic after all.

In his book *The Rise and Fall of Strategic Planning*,[1] Henry Mintzberg uses the metaphor of a potter at the wheel, where strategy is the clay. The key to the potter's craft is the intimate connection between thought and action: guiding the clay, responding to its shape, bringing experience and knowledge to the task while looking to the future, sensing rather than analyzing, and learning while sculpting the clay. Now we are face-to-face with strategic dreaming. Strategic dreaming, unlike strategic planning, is based mostly on hands-on experience rather than on information.

It might help if you think of strategic dreaming as strategic mapping. A strategic map is different from a highway map that says "this way" or "turn here." Strategic mapping is topographical mapping, filling in the hazards, terrain, contour lines of the culture, canyons, streams, and so on. Strategic mapping is not so much a "do this when this occurs" or "avoid this" or "at the next intersection take a right" as it is "Here is the lay of the land." Where you want to go and what you want to accomplish determine which paths might best get you there the safest or the fastest.

Another way to look at strategic mapping is to compare it to jazz. A jazz piece has a basic theme that musicians play all around, improvising as it feels natural to them. The more strategic mappers chart new courses through unfamiliar territory, the more natural it feels to play around with the map, trying new paths and scouting out new initiatives. Some paths will begin to feel more right than others. Over time, strategic mappers begin to smell dead ends (ministries that won't reach people or decisions that will sink the ship) before taking the wrong route. Sure, an enormous amount of thought and planning, as well as endless practice, goes into playing jazz. But in the end, the great jazz musicians have the ability to instantly and unthinkingly sacrifice the best musical score simply because some flash of intuition has suggested a better sound. They have learned how to improvise on the fly.

At the outset, strategic mappers may not have much more than a starting point and a desired destination in mind before setting out on the journey. If the journey is one that has been taken before, some parts of the map may be drawn in already, but not in detail. On the other hand, if the journey is one that has never before been taken, like our situation today, the map is mostly blank between the point of departure and the destination. As the explorers begin to get acquainted with the landscape and the wildlife, they make notes about which paths to take so others can follow (that's what this book wants to do for you). The more people who take the journey, the better the map is drawn. As better equipment is invented, the more detailed the map becomes. Over time, a detailed map to the future emerges for less-adventurous leaders to follow (but we're not there yet in these hard times). We hope the map we will offer you in this book covers the terrain and charts as good a course as can be charted at this point in the journey.

Like explorers, most strategic mappers learn best on the job. The challenges that confront them and the way they handle those situations become their primary learning lab. They may be well educated and terribly smart, but if they are not capable of "adaptive-on-the-journey learning," they wind up spinning their wheels in some dead-end ministry or, worse yet, being eaten alive by one of the many beasts that occupy the jungle culture.

Therefore, strategic dreamers are constantly on the lookout for newer, faster, and better ways to do ministry in a rapidly changing world. They can change course on a dime when they realize the path they are on isn't going anywhere. When mapping a trail through the wilderness, you don't stop to consider if this is the way it's always been done or if you are following procedure. You just make a decision: this trail or that path?— anywhere beats being lost.

MOVING ON

This book will examine each of the hard times rules and share the "how to" of doing strategic dreaming during hard times. Strategic dreaming is not easy. You will be led by God to make some hard decisions. You may have to let some people go. We will help you decide who those people are. You may have to redirect how you spend what money you do have. We will help you see the wisdom in strategically redirecting your budget. You may have to add staff during hard times; you will know if you need to do that once you finish this book.

So it's time to decide. Is the glass half full; or is the glass half empty? How you approach hard times makes a whale of a difference. Read on and discover.

SUGGESTED READING

The Art of the Long View, by Peter Schwartz. Doubleday (1996), 272 pp.

Note
1. Henry Mintzberg. *The Rise and Fall of Strategic Planning* (New York: The Free Press, 1994).

THREE

NOW'S THE TIME TO RETURN TO THE BASICS

One of the benefits of hard times is that smart Christians are forced to examine what they are doing and return to the basics of what made their church great in the first place.

THE PARABLE OF THE MUNCHING SHEEP

The problem is most of our churches have wandered so far from the basics we wouldn't know what's basic and what's not if they bit us in the butt. Most churches remind us of the Parable of the Munching Sheep we developed some time ago. My (BE) first church was in sheep country so I spent a lot of time helping ranchers with their sheep. I soon discovered sheep have a habit of getting so involved in feeding themselves that they munch along for hours without ever looking up to see where they are. All goes well as long as the sheep munch in their own pasture. But if someone leaves a gate open, sheep will munch their way out of the pasture and onto the adjacent highway. There they could be run over by an eighteen-wheeler without even knowing what hit them.

Many Christians do the same. We munch our way so far from our roots that we don't realize how far we have removed ourselves from what we once were and what once made us great. Our greatness is only a memory. As the Scriptures say, "you have left your first love" (Revelation 2:4 NASB).

This chapter is designed to help us see the need for refocusing on the basics that keep a church strong.

Accountability Question: Are you going to be one of those smart leaders who lead your church to return to the basics? Do you know what made your church great in the first place? Once you pinpoint what made you great in the past and begin to focus on it, you may find your glass isn't half empty or half full, but that it "overflows" (Psalm 23:5 NASB).

BURN THE MAP, DISCONNECT THE GPS, AND GET A COMPASS

I (BTB) presumed my GPS was infallible. I presumed it would get me from Point A to Point B without getting me lost, but there I sat in my rented car by the side of the road somewhere in southern Missouri. I was simply trying to get to Little Rock, but according to my GPS, I couldn't get there from where I sat. "You are not on a road" the voice said over and over and over again. And yet, there I was on the side of the main highway that I *thought* was taking me to my next consultation. Even the map said I was in the right place.

> If we aren't sure where we are, and we don't remember from whence we came, how do we get back to the basics of our faith?

Here's a news flash—maps and GPS systems aren't reliable in the jungle culture. The jungle culture changes too often for static maps to be of much value, and the jungle overhead is far too dense for a satellite's signal to penetrate. When you add hard times to the cultural shift going on, you see the impending problem. If we aren't sure where we are, and we don't remember from whence we came, how do we get back to the basics of our faith?

In tough times maps are rendered useless. In both the church and the business world, the maps we have relied on have been strategic plans. The problem with a map or a strategic plan is that they're created with one eye on the past and one eye on what is expected. When tough times come crashing in, plans based on an alternate expectation are instantly out-moded. And because the jungle culture changes almost daily, most strategic plans are outdated within days after they are drawn up. The only reliable navigating tool in times like these is a compass that points unwaveringly to a destination. Using a compass allows us to carefully pick our way through an ever-changing landscape, sidestepping obstacles, climbing over barriers, and avoiding the pitfalls of long-range plans. Only compasses work in the jungle.

In the national park the navigational tools included a mix-ture of mission, vision, bedrock values, and expected behav-iors. Churches worked hard to develop these instruments and some actually used them. We're suggesting, however, that in hard times even these instruments are too cumbersome and time-consuming. Hard times demand a much simpler instrument.

The compass is the most basic of navigation tools, and when tough times come our way, the most practical, efficient, and effective tool is the most basic. Just as the success of any sports team depends first on a commitment to the effective practice of the basics, so too with the church. When the church embraces and embodies the most basic practices of the faith, the church is strengthened and becomes increasingly effective.

In hard times any effective compass points to only two things:

- Doing less means more.
- Jesus is the North Star of any effective compass.

IN HARD TIMES LESS MEANS MORE

It may sound strange, but if your church wants to do well in hard times, it needs to begin by doing less. Less is more in hard times. The more your church puts its time, energy, and money into a few basics, the better the chance it has to remain strong through difficult times.

One of the churches I have consulted with over their eleven-year history provides worship opportunities for around 7,000 twenty-somethings every weekend. During the weeknights, however, the place is mostly dark. They've learned the less you do and the more focused you are on what you do, the more likely the church is to grow. They focus on two things— (1) worship for adults, children, and youth and (2) small groups in the home. Of course, they do other ministries, but it is the bread-and-butter ministries that make or break their church. We could say the same for most of the thriving churches we've worked with over the years. Only a handful of ministries makes or breaks a church.

JESUS IS YOUR COMPASS FOR RECOVERING THE BASICS

Simply put, Jesus is the North Star of any church navigation system that has a chance of working in a jungle culture complicated by hard times. We're not talking about a generic god that could appeal to anyone or arrive at any destination but about the singularity of Jesus Christ. No one in the jungle knows which god you are referring to since there are so many. Sharing the God Jesus Christ is the primary reason churches exist.

Most churches are declining because they have forgotten what business they are in. They have "left [their] first love" (Revelation 2:4 NASB). Declining churches are afraid to talk passionately about Jesus Christ. They are afraid of not being inclusive. They don't want to invade anyone else's space. As a result, they say little or nothing about Jesus and the fire goes out of their ministry. Without offering Jesus the church has nothing to offer and the church ceases to be a church.

In a recent tour stop[1] I (BTB) was speaking on how to share the Good News with a non-Christian. I was explaining how in today's world Christians have to begin where the other person is rather than with the Bible, but in time you have to introduce them to Jesus. A lady in her early fifties raised her hand and said, "Don't you think it is sort of presumptuous of Christians to think that Jesus is any more important than Mohammad?" And she was at a workshop on evangelism!

We're convinced the number one issue facing Protestantism today is the missing answer to Jesus' question, "Who do you say that I am?" (Matthew 16:15). Without a focus on Jesus Christ, it's easy to be content with shuffling the deck chairs around on the *Titanic* or soothing our consciences by clinging to the "righteous remnant" theory (i.e., the smaller the church becomes, the more faithful it is). Without Jesus Christ, our congregations are nothing more than clubs on the lookout for just enough new dues-paying members to help support their programs and keep their buildings open.

On the other hand, we must find ways to profess Jesus Christ as Lord without being bigots. We must never allow our acknowledgment of Jesus Christ to become our only basis of fellowship. Not an easy combination, but we find it in every church that is growing spiritual giants.

Sadly, far too many churches actually organize themselves around this loss of passion for Jesus. Instead of organizing to spread the gospel, they organize to run the institution. In effect they circle the wagons and focus on organizational correctness and effectiveness. And in hard times they circle the wagons even tighter, ensuring a bad outcome.

It is not unusual for key leaders to spend most, if not all, of their time working within the church's premises, attending committee meetings and membership functions. Too many church members find their sense of "belonging" within the church building instead of the community called the church. Going to meetings and preserving church facilities is the number one rival to the First Commandment, let alone the Great Commandment.

Healthy churches focus on transforming people and society rather than on the well-being of the clergy and laity. For example, for two centuries my denomination's (BE) unwritten goal has been to "spread scriptural holiness throughout the land and to reform a nation." The only way my denomination will return to effectiveness is if we organize once again to spread scriptural holiness and reform a nation rather than organizing to provide clergy financial support as we do now.

But most churches have such a rusty compass that it does not point them to the few things that will help a church remain strong during hard times. Just one example: Most churches try to start a contemporary worship service on a shoestring. Launching a new service—or a new church—is one of the primary, innovative ministries in which today's people can experience God, yet it seldom receives the lion's share of the resources (staff, time, prayer, and money). A large church's leader told me (BTB) they did not have the funds to do a contemporary service the right way, so they were not going to do it. In the next breath he mentioned the five hundred thousand dollars they had just spent on remodeling the organ. Who in their right mind or with a heart for Jesus would think remodeling an organ has anything to do with the future of a church in hard times? No one!

With such a shallow commitment to following Jesus, church members place their faith in "their" buildings and demand "their" pastor be "their" personal chaplain. They expect to be served rather than to serve the living Christ. The good news of the gospel becomes "their" personal and private property, and the church, the pastor, and the programs of the church exist primarily for them. They have a misguided vision of what it means to be part of the body of Christ. They think the body of Christ refers only to "their" church; any encroachment on "their" territory is met with resistance. And when hard times fall on them, they retreat deeper within the four walls of the sanctuary.

Church leaders, it's time to find God's passion for your life! Stop what you're doing long enough to listen to what God has to say. Stop doing all those extraneous ministries. Give your people time to breathe. Take time out if necessary. Go off in the wilderness if necessary. Tell the church to cancel all of the meetings for the next six months and to gather for prayer instead. Do whatever you have to do, but get a vision of Jesus! A life-changing vision is what causes church leaders to accept change. And we're not talking about a vision statement that is arrived at by hours of meetings. We're talking about a God-given vision that is birthed in the passion of the spiritual leader.

WE ARE A SENT CHURCH

When Jesus is the North Star of the compass, there is only one way to define the church—it is a group of "sent" people. Jesus said to them, "Peace be with you; as the Father has sent Me, I also send you" (John 20:21, NASB). Whatever else we can say about the church, every church must be a "sent" church if it's going to be an authentic church rather than a club. The church exists for those who have not yet heard the unbelievable good news of God in Christ. Mission and evangelism are the total identity of the church. Theology follows missiology. Churches don't need a mission or evangelism committee because that is what the church is.

> In every time, but especially in hard times, the church needs to spend all of its time, energy, and money on thrusting itself outward into the world.

This means the biblical church is always faced outward to the world and what God is doing in the world. It is never turned inward on itself. Now, we know the problem with the vast majority of churches in the United States—most churches are turned inward, spending most of their time on their members. We're suggesting just the opposite as the starting point. In every time, but especially in hard times, the church needs to spend all of its time, energy, and money on thrusting itself outward into the world.

GETTING PRACTICAL

We know that much of what we've said may seem esoteric and impractical. "Cancel all the meetings for six months, indeed. Who does he think we are?" And yet, this is exactly the problem. Unless the church is willing to be serious about finding their True North, everything we've said or will say might as well be shredded.

I (BTB) have been coaching and consulting with a church for over a year now. This church has been confronted with a number of significant changes during that time and has many more to face. However, the governing council now spends much of their time together studying and praying rather than discussing and planning. Indeed, during a number of meetings, they've not gotten around to business at all.

We know of a pastor who was committed to helping the church rediscover its North Star, so he took a whole month off just to fast and pray and listen. Another pastor of a very large church took several months off for the same reason. In both cases, they came back not only refreshed but able to lead from a stable spiritual center.

So what would happen, really, if you converted all your meetings for six months to prayer meetings? Do you really believe your current meetings are what keeps the church "going"? If you'll take the risk and make prayer the agenda rather than the parenthesis, your compass might actually start working again.

MOVING ON

In the ensuing chapters we will suggest that only a handful of ministries can help a church remain strong during hard times, and some ministries can always be cut out of the budget without harming the mission.

SUGGESTED READING

A Second Resurrection, by Bill Easum. Abingdon Press (2007), 126 pp.

High-Voltage Spirituality, by Bill Tenny-Brittian. Chalice Press (2006), 192 pp.

Note

1. To see the Hitchhikers Guide to Evangelism tour go to http://easum bandy.com/upcoming_events/hitchhiker_tour_2009/

FOUR

THE HARD TIMES
BUDGET FORMULA

Charities are among the first organizations to find their revenue drying up in hard times. And toward the top of the list of charities people can cut giving to is their church. In hard times giving to the church always goes down. So again we ask, "Does the glass appear to be half full, half empty, or running over?" How you answer that question determines whether or not you can dream strategically.

> If you learn how to spend strategically you can actually achieve more with less!

If you believe the glass is half full, you know you'd better get your rear in gear because during hard times people are far more likely to return to church than they are in good times, and the church needs to be ready to welcome them. On the other hand, if you believe the glass is half empty, you are likely to hunker down with a bunker mentality and miss the parade of people. But if you believe your glass is running over, even in hard times, you probably have the passion to overcome whatever may come because Jesus is guiding and driving you forward.

Now is not the time to hunker down and indiscriminately slash costs. Now's the time to do strategic dreaming. You see, the issue is not always whether or not we have enough money. Even in good times the issue is seldom how much money we have. The issue, especially during hard times, is how strategically we spend the money we do have. *If you learn how to spend strategically, you can actually achieve more with less!*

STRATEGIC DREAMING ABOUT SPENDING DURING HARD TIMES

So what does it mean to strategically dream about the way a church spends its money? In order to answer this question, we have to ask and answer a previous question—what is the prime directive of every church?

The last words the church remembers Jesus saying were "Go be my witnesses in Jerusalem, Judea, Samaria, and to the ends of the world." He pretty much laid out the marching orders of every church. As we said earlier, but it bears repeating—the role of the church is to be a witness to Jesus Christ—everywhere.

The word "witness" means more than just giving testimony about Jesus. It also means "to be a martyr," to give one's life for a cause. Strategic leaders spend what money they do have on things that allow the church to be the best witness to Jesus Christ it can be. And that never means hunkering down during bad times. It means redirecting how we spend our money so the story continues to be told.

Another of Jesus' last remembered words was "Go make disciples." Everything a church does should be directed toward making and growing disciples. We need to examine our budgets to ensure the lion's share goes to making disciples and being a witness to Jesus Christ.

So what does this mean in practical terms?

During hard times we've found it's helpful to divide strategic dreaming about the spending of money into two categories—what should always be cut and what should always be increased. Using these two categories makes it easier to analyze a budget without the normal wringing of the hands. Over the years of consulting we've answered these questions in a methodical manner. We've found the following formula to be effective in the good times, but even *more* effective in hard times.

Take a good, long look at the following formula.

The Hard Times Budget Formula

Always Increase:

Worship
Children's Ministry
Evangelism
Marketing
Continuing Education
Volunteer Ministries
Small Groups
Spiritual Formation

Always Cut:

Office Personnel
Missions
Youth Program
Nonessential Ministries
Money in the Bank

Accountability Question: How did you feel while looking at the Hard Times Budget Formula? You probably don't like what you see, do you? But let us ask you—if you keep doing what you've been doing, can you really expect the outcome to be any different? Do you really believe that cutting the budget and simply not spending money will help you emerge a stronger church on the other side of hard times? We hope not. But that's the way many churches will choose to address hard times. It's our hope you're not one of them.

> Two of the hardest decisions churches have to make is cutting and redirecting the budget and releasing personnel.

A hard-times economy requires leaders who make wise, strategic decisions. Encourage your leaders to spend time in prayer asking God for guidance in how to spend what money they do receive in 2010–11. Don't be fooled; nine out of ten churches will receive less money in 2010–11 than they did in 2009. But, if they get strategic, they can wind up achieving more with less. Remember, with God all things are possible. So go for it. Redirect your money *now* into those ministries that will help you achieve God's prime directive for the church. In the following chapters we will examine what this means.

CUTTING AND REDIRECTING THE BUDGET STRATEGICALLY

In hard times, hard decisions have to be made if a church wants to remain strong and to emerge even stronger on the other side of the difficulties. Two of the hardest decisions churches have to make is cutting and redirecting the budget and releasing personnel. Most churches avoid these like the plague.

> Remember, we're not talking about simply cutting the budget. We're encouraging you to take action now while you still have enough money to redirect the funds you do have to those "Always Increase" ministries.

SEVERAL RULES PREVAIL IN HARD TIMES

- Start making strategic adjustments to your budget the moment it's apparent that hard times are upon you. Don't wait until things get so bad you are forced to make adjustments. That way you will still have enough money to do what is necessary to thrive.

- Strategically adjust your budget on a quarterly basis rather than annually. If you have an annual budget, forget it. Waiting that long to make budget changes will be devastating. Instead, establish a cash income flow chart for the past three years. Determine the average percentage of income for each month of the year during that time. This will allow you to compare this month to the average of the same month for the last three years. This way, you'll know after the first quarter of the year where you are likely to be at the end of the year if you don't do something different. For example, if at the end of the first quarter you should have received 19.8 percent of your income and you only received 18.8 percent, you know you are 1 percent short for the first quarter. Probably the same will hold true for the rest of the year, making you a total of 4 percent short for the year.

In a year of major economic downturn, however, you can probably expect the results will get worse, so double whatever percentage you originally arrived at. This way you have a much safer picture of what you need to cut and redirect.

- Redirect all the money you can into the "Always Increase" ministries that have a chance of pulling you through the hard times. You see, we're not just asking you to cut the budget. We're asking you to cut the budget early enough and deep enough so that even though you have less money, you still have money that can be redirected into the "Always Increase" column of ministries.

- Cut out all the fluff such as outside groups using your facilities for free (this used to be a way to grow a church; it isn't today). Also cut all meetings at the church and hold them in homes to save on fuel costs. In fact, we would ask you to cut all of your meetings, period. Doing so will free up more people to serve in the areas where you will have to make deep staff cuts. And don't be tempted to switch to "virtual" meetings so you can still keep everything under control. The church isn't under your control in the first place. And meetings, virtual or not, are time and energy wasters. Put a leader, not a committee, in charge of a ministry, and you'll get lots more done.

- If you have any money saved up for a raining day, let us remind you, in case you hadn't noticed: it's raining. Hard times are the time to spend all of that rainy day money on the "Always Increase" ministries. Don't be one of those churches that close with money in the bank.

Most churches hunker down and try to scrimp and scrape by until the crisis is so severe there isn't any money left over to redirect and resurrect the church. They wait too long. Remember, we're not talking about simply cutting the budget. We're encouraging you to take action now while you still have enough money to redirect the funds you do have to those "Always Increase" ministries. It's far more important how you spend your money than how much money you have. So please don't wait. If you find yourself in hard times, start strategically cutting and redirecting before the only option you have left is slashing the budget and closing the doors if the crisis doesn't go away very soon.

MOVING ON

In the remaining chapters we will explore the ins and outs of the Hard Times Budget. Let's begin with what must be cut in order to increase our spending in the key areas that will help the church thrive during hard times.

FIVE

BUDGET ITEMS YOU ALWAYS CUT IN HARD TIMES

W e know you are going to hate this chapter. We also know you may not heed its wisdom. But you will ignore it at your peril. If you keep spending your money the way you have been spending it, you'll continue getting what you've been getting, and since you'll have less money to spend, you'll find your church digging a very deep financial hole.

The Hard Times Budget Formula

Always Cut:

Office Personnel
Missions
Youth Program
Nonessential Ministries
Money in the Bank

So here are some things you can cut out of a budget to make room for redirecting money into ministries that should always be increased.

CUT YOUR OFFICE PERSONNEL

The best place to start redirecting the budget is with office personnel, because in most churches over two hundred in worship, it is one of the most bloated areas. There is an old axiom—paper expands to fill the size of the desk. The same is true about office personnel; the number of people will expand to fill the space. It's rare to find a staff that thinks it has enough secretarial help.

Most established churches we've worked with over the years have far too many personnel in the office. One church had a $150,000 budget and was paying someone $18,000 a year to oversee the budget. Another church had a $2 million budget, 5,000 members, 900 average attendance, only five full-time pastoral/program staff, no money in the budget for evangelism or advertising, and twelve full-time people working in the office. Any wonder it was dying? You may think these are exceptions, but the fact is, we've found excessive office employees to be the rule.

> No one person, let us repeat, *no one person* is more important than the mission of the church.

So the first place to do some strategic dreaming is to ask, "Who in the office can we survive without and it not cost us momentum?" Pray about it and write down the names. Everyone on that list should be let go.

Accountability Question: Are you willing to attempt this cutting? Do you need to gather some allies in order to make it happen? Will it jeopardize your job? Are you willing to let the church go down the tubes to save your job?

We know. You think we're cold-hearted. It may seem that way, but it really isn't. It's a strategic way to redirect money into those ministries that will allow you to remain strong and emerge on the other side of the crises a stronger church. People in the office seldom have anything whatsoever to do with the growth of the church. And when you are in hard times, increasing the number of people in worship has to be one of your priorities. So the quicker you become really lean in the office, the quicker you will have money to shift into the "Always Increase" ministries.

When it comes to releasing staff, most church leaders make one huge mistake. Especially when it comes to long-term employees, they find it difficult to put the overall mission of God's church before a human being, but that is exactly what we're asking you to do. No one person, let us repeat, *no one person* is more important than the mission of the church. As a church leader, and especially as the pastor, you've been asked to care for and to lead the church. The church is a called out *people*, not a called out *person*. So take out a very sharp pencil and start cutting. Later you'll be glad you did.

In one of my (BE) first churches, I experienced this reluctance to fire staff first-hand. The church had a secretary who had been there more than thirty years. She was a jewel. The only problem was she couldn't do anything anymore other than talk on the phone (but boy was she skilled at that). One afternoon the pastor called me in to tell me he was doing away with the youth budget. I inquired why he made that decision. He responded, "We have to cut the youth budget so we can hire another person to do the secretary's work." When I asked if they were letting the secretary go, he said, "We can't do that; she's family." I couldn't believe it. They were putting an individual ahead of the mission. They were allowing a staff person to become a mission project rather than being on a mission. It's hard for church people to take the strategic step of letting personnel go. But if you don't, you are choosing to sacrifice the very mission of the church.

Some helpful hints about cutting and redirecting office costs into ministries that can make the church solvent again are:

- A good rule of thumb for secretaries is one full-time person for every three to five full-time pastoral/program staff, which means very few churches in the United States needs more than one secretary, if that. Notice we said three to five. If you have two or fewer full-time pastoral/program staff members, you should be able to get along with volunteer staffing.

- At one point the church I served had eleven hundred in worship and only one secretary, but dozens of volunteers. If you have any retired people in your church, you have a built-in pool of volunteers if you are willing to train them. I (BE) remember consulting with Community Church of Joy in Phoenix. The person answering the phone was a volunteer who had been trained in how to direct calls to the appropriate person, and the chief custodian was running the prison ministry at no charge to the church.

- Weekly or monthly newsletters haven't been important for some time now. They can be replaced easily with email or by word of mouth. When something important is about to happen, instead of doing a regular newsletter, send out an e-mail to those who have email and a written notice to those who don't, but only if it involves the entire church. And don't forget the changing technology. If you're not collecting the cell phone numbers of your under-thirties, you're missing out on their primary communications tool: text messaging.

- If you have more than one secretary, use a secretarial pool instead of assigning secretaries to program people. It has been repeatedly proven that a secretarial pool, from which all staff draw, requires fewer secretaries and accomplishes more. Ministry needs are not the same all the time in every area of the church. There are times when one area is so busy the secretary has more to do than is possible. Then there are times when that same secretary has to look for things to do. Secretarial pools balance out the workload of each secretary and save money.

- Unless you are in a church of over two thousand in worship, the pastor doesn't need his or her own secretary. Remember, pastor, the mission is more important than any one person.

- Cleaning services can be replaced with organized and coordinated volunteers. Fellowship and belongingness is the upside of such a decision. At New Hope Fellowship in Oahu, many new members begin their first "serving" opportunity by cleaning the restrooms. Even the Hawaii Superior Court judge and his family began their service in the church by "cleaning the toilets for Jesus."
- If your budget is under $700,000, you don't need a paid treasurer, financial secretary, or bookkeeper to handle the money. Instead, all you need is three people to count the money, a person to write checks, and a person to sign the checks. At the church where I (BE) was pastor for twenty-four years, we used volunteers until we had a budget of just under $700,000 and it worked fine. It's also less expensive to outsource the bookkeeping than it is to have a paid person on staff. And there are other benefits as well. Outsourced bookkeepers almost never begin to act as if the church's bank account is "their" money.
- During hard times, forgo any financial audits. Have one done as soon as things return to normal. But ensure you have safeguards in place, such as multiple people counting the money, or an approval process for larger checks.
- The following staff seldom pays for themselves except in a church of more than two thousand in worship, so if your church is smaller and has any of the following you should probably let them go.

1. Communications Director. A myth prevails in many churches that if we just had someone in charge of communications, everyone would know what is going on all the time. Nonsense. Most people don't care what is going on as long as worship excels and their small group is fulfilling. And those who complain are either saying that no one wants to attend whatever it is they are offering or else they are wanting to be consulted on any and every decision the church might make.

2. Activities Director. More and more churches have an expensive fellowship hall or recreation facility they are trying to justify by ensuring the facility is used as much as possible. So they hire an activities director to try and keep its calendar full. But ask yourself two questions: "Is the ministry actually growing the church? And has anyone become a Christian as a result?" Depending on your answers, you know what to do.

3. Web Designer/IT. Websites are important today. But unless you are over two thousand in worship, ask some of your youth to take over this ministry. In lieu of payment, offer to buy them a software program they want but can't afford to purchase. If you doubt your youth can handle it, ask to see some of the YouTube videos they're producing. If they can do YouTube, they can handle your website easily.

4. Assistants for Children and Youth Directors. Unless you have more than three hundred children or one hundred fifty youth in regular attendance at one time, you don't need these personnel in the first place, so let them go.

5. Bell Choir Leader and Children's Choir Leader. These are nice ministries but they do nothing significant for the overall mission. At best they are important for the handful of people who participate in them, especially handbells. These ministries can be accomplished with unpaid leaders.

- Require staff to use e-mail and texting as forms of communicating and avoid using paper. This practice saves money and time—but only if you don't print out everything you get. Think twice before printing. If you have trouble sorting through your e-mails and sms texts, develop a better folder system in your e-mail software.
- Organize as many groups as you can to alternate doing the custodial work around the church.

CUT MOST FOREIGN AND LOCAL MISSIONS

One local church we worked with during the late 1980s in Texas during the oil bust was hemorrhaging in worship attendance to the point that if the decline continued another decade it would have to close. Their worship budget, including personnel, was just under $15,000 in a budget of over $350,000. When we suggested they redirect some of their money to hire a good worship leader and lead singer, they said they couldn't find that much money. Yet even though their budget had declined by almost 50 percent over the previous four years, they had not cut their mission budget and were giving some 40 to 50 percent of their existing budget to missions. One of the solutions to their situation was to cut the mission budget to zero and invest that money in worship and evangelistic outreach to the community. Doing that would give them a chance to survive the economic downturn during those terrible five years in Texas. When the downturn turned around, they could then reinstate the mission budget. Of course, even thinking about such a change was too much for their leaders to endure. After several months deliberating, they decided against making the cut. Two years later they cut their mission budget anyway because the church had declined to the point they had to cut something and the mission budget was all that was left to cut. You can cut now and increase your chances of a successful conclusion to these troubled times, or you can cut later because there's nothing left to throw overboard as your *Titanic* sinks. Your choice.

It pains us to even suggest cutting your mission budget to the bone, but in hard times, it must be done. It doesn't make sense to send money away to help some other mission when the mission at home is in jeopardy. In hard times it's necessary to shore up the home front so there will be long-term money for missions. You will do well to cut this portion of your budget to zero until you make it through the hard times. When things return to normal, you can rebuild your mission budget to what it was.

Now consider this—by cutting the mission budget you can easily do what you need to do anyway—focus on the mission in your backyard and provide ministries for people who may have been so devastated by the economic downturn they simply can't afford to give to the church but still have the desire to help.

CUT THE YOUTH BUDGET

We know; you've probably been told the youth are the future of your church. Not so! They are the future of someone else's church. Not yours. Most of them will grow up and move on to some other city.

Now, we're not saying you should not introduce youth to Christ or mentor them for the future. You should. The foundation you give them should last a lifetime. But don't be fooled—*they are not the future of your church*. If you continue thinking they are, you may not get through the hard times. We're also not encouraging you to cut the youth program, only to cut the youth budget funds.

We suggest you do four things with the youth program.

- Cut the budget to zero unless you have more than one hundred and fifty youth in regular attendance every week and then you need paid staff.
- Do not have a full-time youth director unless you have at least one hundred youth in regular attendance during the week. With fewer than that, you don't need a full-time youth director. If you have more than fifty youth in regular attendance, find a very part-time person who can gather some strong laypeople to help give guidance to the program. If you have fewer than fifty youth, there is no reason the pastor can't lead the youth program for a time with the help of strong laypeople. When our youth program was small, my wife and I (BE) were responsible for the youth program so we could direct money to the one place that makes more difference than any other program person you can hire—a worship leader. One of the biggest

mistakes small churches make is for their first hire to be a youth director. Don't just avoid that mistake in hard times—rectify it.

- Drop all subsidies to the youth program. Subsidies are any form of money allocated in the budget to the youth program other than staff salary. It's not uncommon for churches to spend more money on youth trips than on worship. Unlike children, youth are perfectly capable of raising their own money, so it makes no sense to give them subsidies. Besides, the national park trick of taking youth on an extra-special youth trip to somewhere far away to do some kind of service project they could do in their own backyard no longer grows youth groups.

> Instead of emphasizing entertainment ministry, shift the focus to disciple-making.

- Stop treating your youth like they're Beaver and Wally Cleaver (or even Greg or Marsha Brady). They're more sophisticated and spiritually aware than that. Teach them to pray. Teach them to share their faith. Teach them to make a difference. Help them answer the Ultimate Question for themselves ("What is it about your relationship with Jesus that your neighbors can't live without?"). Encourage them to hold each other accountable for the spiritual disciplines and for their behaviors. Invite them to do real ministry within the church regularly, not just on Youth Sunday. Not only will you discover that this will cost a lot less money, you'll actually grow spiritual giants at a young age.

CUT NONESSENTIAL MINISTRIES

Over the years churches pile up many ministries that once might have been effective and needed but over time have become irrelevant. In hard times these ministries have to go because they eat up time, energy, and money. Remember, the key here is to ask, "Can we survive without this ministry?" If your answer is "Yes," drop it. By doing so, you'll be in a better position to move from surviving to thriving. Here are a few examples of non-essential ministries we've seen over the years (we know, there are many more).

- Most meetings that require laypeople to spend hours at church making decisions that could be made by either a few people or a single key leader in much less time. Ask "Which meetings can we cancel indefinitely and it will not hurt our growth?" Cancel them. It will free up some lay people to help with ministries that you were paying people to do; save on utilities and cleaning; and free up the paid staff to have more time to build up themselves spiritually. Remember, two key things never happen in meetings: no one ever becomes a Christian; and no one ever grows in their faith. I (BE) have seen more people lost to the church because the first thing the church did was put them on a committee. So cancel all the committee meetings you can without jeopardizing your mission. You will be surprised how many meetings you can do without.
- Kitchen Ministry. Many churches have come to enjoy having in-house kitchen personnel to provide lunch for the staff and meals in the evening during church functions. This service is a luxury a church cannot afford in hard times.
- The Parish Nurse is a program that few churches need in good times. It is a luxury in hard times unless your church is located in an area with very high unemployment or a high percentage of senior citizens.
- Any weeknight program that isn't integral to the lifeblood of the congregation. Move your Wednesday evening programs (and all the rest) from the church building into members' homes. You'll discover that when the same ministry is relocated into a home, the intimacy and fellowship will increase exponentially. This is the heart of

the church in good times. In hard times, open and transparent fellowship is the lifeblood for many.

- In-house food banks. Except in a few urban settings, food banks are rarely a door into the church for its clients. Instead of putting time and money into your church food bank, donate all your foodstuffs to the local, secular food bank and then shift your volunteers to work there. By doing so, you'll immediately make it a Christian ministry because of your presence. Besides, you'll find more opportunities to share your faith in word and deed with the unchurched and unconnected in these settings.
- Rummage Sales, Christmas Bazaars, Fish Fries, and so forth. These are killer time and energy wasters and bring little income or goodwill from the community. I (BTB) know of a prominent church in a metro area that was struggling and couldn't grow. We went into the local community to see if we could discover the church's reputation. It grieved me terribly when I heard time after time, "Oh, that's the church with the big yard sale every year." If that's the reputation you want, then keep on having rummage sales and chili cook-offs.

REDIRECT MONEY IN THE BANK

Most churches have some money socked away for a rainy day. They cling to it as if it will be their salvation sometime in the distant future. They do almost anything to keep from spending a dime of the money. If they do spend some, they spend interest only.

The fear of spending money is so great that we've seen churches close with money in the bank. I (BE) remember one church that closed its doors for good while having $100,000-plus in a fund designated for chancel furnishings. Don't make that mistake. Now is the time to pull out all the stops. It's not the time to count pennies. It's the time to strategically invest in things that will make the most difference in your future. So, if you have money in the bank, now is the time to spend it all in one fell swoop.

MOVING ON

We know this chapter may have been a bitter pill to swallow. Some of your most prized ministries have been assaulted. We didn't do that lightly. As important as those ministries are, they will not determine the life or death of a church. When things get better, we recommend you begin funneling money back into some of these ministries. But be careful—some of those ministries are married to tradition rather than discipleship.

Accountability Question: Are you up for making these hard cuts? Will you discuss them with your key leaders? You may be surprised at their response.

Before we take a look at the ministries you always want to increase in hard times, we need to address the feeling you're probably experiencing at the moment, especially after reading this chapter. We want to talk about the beast that always rears its ugly head during hard times.

SUGGESTED READING

People Are Being Programmed to Death, www.BillEasum.com (blog).

SIX

OVERCOMING THE HARD-TIMES BEAST

Over the past few months Jim's had a hard time sleeping. All he's been able to think of is that his job is in jeopardy and his pension has eroded. He is nearing retirement and knows he won't have enough time left to recoup his losses. Much of what he worked for all his life is disappearing. He's cut back in every area of his life to try to mitigate his fears. HBO is gone. He's back on dial-up. He cancelled the family vacation. And he can't remember the last time he had a steak. Jim is not a happy camper and Tums have become his favorite candy.

Jim faithfully serves his church as the chair of the Finance Committee. And guess what? The finances of the church don't look much different from what Jim worries about at home every night. Jim brings his fears and his despair with him into the committee. All Jim can think to do is lead the committee to slash the budget to bare bones and hunker down. But such action guarantees the church will become weaker on the other side of the hard times.

The problem becomes worse because one of the people on the Finance Committee is facing bankruptcy and another has just been told the bank will no longer carry his mortgage. The combination of Jim and these two members of the committee make for a half-empty glass outlook when it comes to the church's finances.

Like so many churches during hard times, Jim and his committee are ruled by fear. They are afraid that both their lives and the life of their church are going down the tubes. As a result, none of them is capable of dreaming strategically.

Jim and his committee are not alone. The whole world is locked in the grip of the Hard-times Beast: fear.

We can understand our nation going berserk. We've been a wealthy nation for a long time. We also understand some individuals going off half-cocked and acting insane when the market crashes. But Christians should never be overcome with fear.

A CULTURE OF FEAR

During tough times, fear becomes the Hard-times Beast that destroys churches, families, and friends. Fear can possess us only when we shut faith, hope, and love out of our lives. The moment leaders quit demonstrating fearless, compassionate leadership, fear creeps into the church. It must be conquered if the church is to remain strong.

Fear does strange things to people. It makes even the most intelligent person do dumb things. It causes sane people to put a gun to their head, nations to go to war, friends to turn on each other, and intelligent church leaders to slash the budget.

> This culture of fear is one of your biggest worries over the next couple of years.

Left unchecked, fear can become a contagious addiction that paralyzes the human spirit. Once Jim shared with the committee his deep-seated fear, the group was eager to slash and burn the budget with little regard for the consequence. All they could think of was survival.

The longer fear rules, the more likely the church is to develop a culture of fear. A culture of fear is an environment in which fear is the primary source of energy. In contrast to a culture of fear, a culture of faith finds its energy source in strategic dreaming. What can be is always more important than what is.

This culture of fear is one of your biggest worries over the next couple of years. If fear is allowed to remain the central focus of the church, the congregation will become so traumatized that total stagnation will set in and no one will have the capacity to strategically dream. Without a dream, the church falls into a downward spiral.

One of the worst things about a culture of fear is that it saps all of the leaders' energy. It saps their power source and renders them virtually helpless when it comes to taking any kind of positive action. Leaders begin to close ranks and protect what little they have because they fear they will run out of money—so doing nothing and spending less becomes the best offense.

But here is the worst reality about a culture of fear. Fear is the opposite of love. It drives people away from the only thing that can sustain them in hard times—faith. It robs them of any passion for the future and replaces hope with despair. It causes good people to put themselves before the gospel mandates. Fear fills a void in people when their faith is either absent or weak. Left unchecked, a culture of fear replaces love, openness, and creativity. Fanning the flames of fear will lead to your church's demise.

Fear must be driven out, especially in the hardest of times. Sometimes it's even necessary to remind your people they need to take the press and media with a grain of salt because they all hype negative issues. Remember, bad news sells. Their goal is to increase ratings more than to communicate reality. And they know that fear is a potent weapon when trying to capture a market. So wise people don't allow themselves to give in to the Hard-times Beast.

The good news is that we can learn to neutralize fear. The speeches and demeanor of some of the world's greatest leaders—Winston Churchill, FDR, John Kennedy, and Ronald Reagan—were loaded with verbal power that diminished fear. We could take a lesson from them and empower our own speaking with words that neutralize fear. So let's look at some of the ways for Christians to conquer the culture of fear.

NEUTRALIZING THE BEAST

We've said it many times, but it bears repeating. "You can't give what you don't have." During hard times it is imperative that church leaders strengthen themselves spiritually so they can adequately lead the congregation by focusing on the glass running over. Spiritually mature people tend to avoid the fear traps set by the Hard-times Beast.

During these times your congregation is going to need sound, wise, and encouraging leadership. This type of leadership is difficult enough in good times; it is next to impossible in hard times unless God is an essential partner in the plan.

We've found two things necessary to neutralize the Hard-times Beast—keeping leaders spiritually and physically fit and developing the key leaders into spiritual giants.

LEADERS MUST KEEP SPIRITUALLY AND PHYSICALLY FIT

You hear it every time you get on a plane. "In case of pressure loss in the cabin, oxygen masks will drop from an overhead compartment. . . . Please put on your own oxygen mask first before helping children or other passengers." In other words, if you don't take care of yourself, you're going to be of no use to anyone else.

> In hard times the congregation looks for signs of hope in the faces, words, and practices of church leaders.

This is especially true with the leader's spiritual life in hard times. In hard times the congregation looks for signs of hope in the faces, words, and practices of church leaders. This makes it all the more critical for you to be faithful in the spiritual disciplines. Hopefully your life is already calibrated by the following disciplines. They will serve you well in hard times. But if you haven't cultivated them, now is the time to do so.

Prayer

Just about everyone we know "believes" in prayer—but believing in prayer means something different to almost everyone we talk to. Since this is the only communication tool we have to reach God, however, no matter what we "believe" about it, it's the tool we need to be using.

A number of surveys over the years have indicated that clergy in the United States spend only a few minutes a day in prayer—almost 60 percent pray less than fifteen minutes each day. In hard times like these, you must be intentional in your prayer time—both asking and listening. And when you're in unsettled water, it is generally more important to listen than to ask.

We suggest you set aside the first hour or so of every morning for prayer and devotional time with God. During your prayer time listen more than you ask. I (BE) remember one of my good friends telling me one day, "It was when I ran out of things to pray for that I finally heard God speak to me."

Don't let anything rob you of this time. If you have an early appointment, then get up earlier so you can spend time with God. Nothing will calm the culture of fear any better than spending regular time with God.

Keep a journal during this time alone. Write down your fear thoughts; then compare them to some of the great Scripture passages that have sustained you over time. Doing this reveals the folly of fear and power of prayer.

Accountability Question: What is the most significant word/message you heard from God in your listening time this week?

Scripture Reflection

Most folks call this Bible study, but study isn't the goal. Although study is good, when we study the Bible we tend to treat it as a textbook and we focus our minds academically. In hard times, it's more important to spend significant devotional time reading and reflecting on what we've read.

Without going into the specifics of how or why it works, spending regular and intentional time reading and reflecting on Scripture, especially in the Gospels, transforms lives. If the average pastor spends a few minutes daily in prayer, then it's probably a good bet the average pastor spends even less time in Scripture reflection. There are many tools to help you reflect, from journaling to devotional books. If you're at a loss about how to effectively increase your quality time with the Bible, see *High-Voltage Spirituality*, by Bill Tenny-Brittian.[1]

Accountability Question: What did you read in Scripture (pastors, outside of your sermon preparation) this week that sparked a flame in you?

Retreats

There's no question difficult times can drain even the most dedicated spiritual leader. The demands and related stress can be paralyzing. That's why it's more important than ever for you to take some time to get away from it all. We're not talking about a vacation but about time in "a lonely place" where you can have considerable one-on-one time with Jesus. We recommend "Get thee to a nunnery" or a monastery or some other pilgrimage site that calls to your heart and refreshes your soul.

Leave everything behind—your laptop, Blackberry, cell phone, and even your calendar that you desperately need to get under control. Take only your Bible and your journal and don't do any sermon preparation. This is a time for *just* you, your Bible, your journal, and lots of prayer.

We recommend you go on at least a one-day retreat every month and an overnight retreat at least once a quarter. If you can manage a once-a-month overnight, that's even better.

Accountability Question: When was the last time you took a whole day to get away and spend time with God? When is your next scheduled retreat day and where are you going?

Physical Activity

Too many pastors live sedentary lives, which does not serve them well in good times, much less in bad times. When leaders are tired or out of shape, it affects their ability to give the kind of leadership needed in hard times. It's not only about being in shape; apparently when you're physically active, your brain works better. A working mind is more likely to tame the Hard-times Beast than a sedentary one. So, if you're a couch potato or if you're tied to your computer or Blackberry, perhaps it's time to take a membership in the nearby gym, or take up a sport, or just get outside and take a long walk (or a run!).

Accountability Question: When was the last time you had a real workout?

Encouragement

Although we could list many more spiritual practices to help you get your spiritual oxygen mask on, we want to conclude with just one more. In today's culture, encouragement often means giving someone a "brownie button" or an "attaboy." And though praise is a good thing, that's not what we mean by encouragement.

To encourage someone spiritually is to gently invite them to take the "next step" in their faith journey. Sometimes this means asking someone one of the accountability questions you've encountered in this book. Sometimes this means simply asking someone how you can be an encouragement to them. And sometimes it means asking someone how you can pray for them.

I (BTB) often ask pastors, "What would it be like if you got a phone call, e-mail, or text message every couple of days from your congregation asking how they could pray for you this week?" The typical response I get is somewhere between "wishful thinking" and "absolutely amazing." We all need encouragers and, as a reminder, it's one of the key one-anothers of the New Testament: "Encourage one another" (1 Thessalonians 5:11; Hebrews 3:13; Hebrews 10:25). And since followers emulate their leaders, it's imperative the pastor initiates this practice. Especially in hard times, each member of your congregation is in need of spiritual encouragement. And the fact is, they'll not call on others (or you) if you're not modeling the practice yourself.

Accountability Question: Who did you intentionally reach out to this week with a spiritual-journey encouragement?

DEVELOP SPIRITUAL GIANTS

I (BTB) had an experience in a seminar recently where I shared that one of the chief ministries of the church was to develop spiritual giants. Within moments, I was bombarded with "concerns" that the crowd (mostly clergy) wasn't comfortable with the term "spiritual giants." It quickly became clear these concerns were borne from their belief that expecting spiritual maturity of the congregants was too lofty an ideal. In other words, it's better to shoot for spiritual mediocrity.

Mediocrity has been the middle name for the North American church for too long and it's time to do something about that. In hard times, a mediocre faith simply won't cut it. In nature, only the strong survive, but in Christianity, the survivors are those who have "old souls." The old souls are the "Timothys," who have been invited to walk with their Paul, Peter, and Barnabas. And in turn, they have invited their own Timothys to take a faith walk in the Land of Giants.

In hard times, the church has to engage in heroic efforts to create adult spiritual formation opportunities. There are literally hundreds of books, packages, and programs that try to teach adults to be spiritually mature. However, few if any actually achieve this goal. Instead, spiritual giants are raised under the tutelage of formal and informal mentors—the Pauls, Peters, Barnabases, and Timothys of the church. These types of folks are generally found in small numbers in most churches, but they are one of the keys to your future.

- Paul was a spiritual giant developer par excellence. He achieved this feat with a twofold focus. He was both a teacher and a modeler of the faith. Even though he taught a great deal, his teaching was made effective by his modeling. Repeatedly he reminded his readers to live by the pattern of faith he'd modeled for them. In our modern world, we often blow Paul off as an arrogant blowhard, but Paul knew something we've forgotten. Spirituality isn't taught so much as it "rubs off" on us. When people spend time in the presence of spiritual giants, those engaged in the discipleship journey begin to emulate their mentors—their Pauls.

I (BE) experience such mentoring every time I'm in the presence of Wayne Cordeiro, the pastor of New Hope Christian Fellowship in Honolulu. Just to be in his presence makes me a better follower of Christ because of the way Wayne's spirit rubs off on me. If I could, I would spend a day a month just following him around (a guy can dream, can't he?).

Adult faith formation begins with a combination of teaching and conspicuous modeling. The church must develop ministries that pair true spiritual giants with spiritual newbies.

* Peter may have been a teacher and a mentor as well, but we actually have little evidence of this. Instead, Peter excelled in at least one area of spiritual-giant development: he held people accountable for their behaviors. Notice that it's Peter who holds Ananias and Sapphira accountable in Acts 5. It's Peter who goes to the Samaritans to check on their conversion. And it's Peter to whom Paul voluntarily submits for his own accountability.

Accountability in the church has a terrible reputation. Mention the word and images of wagging fingers, furrowed brows, and not-quite-audible whispering dance through our brains. And yet, Peters are absolutely necessary to develop spiritual giants. The problem is we have a lousy understanding of accountability, at least when it comes to the adult spiritual formation part. Remember the section on "encouragement"? Well, effective accountability is similar to the biblical understanding of encouragement—the point is to encourage one another to take the next step and hold them accountable for doing so.

Interestingly, there seems to be an inverse opportunity

for spiritual development in hard times. In times like these, many are ready to take on real change in their lives. They're willing to take the next step in their faith journey, but they're unlikely to take that step if they're not encouraged to do so. Holding people accountable for their own spiritual development is an effective encouragement tool.

Adult faith formation moves from head to hands (behaviors) when encouragement includes accountability questions such as (1) What did you read in Scripture this week that intrigued you? (2) What is the most significant word/message you heard from God in your listening time this week? And (3) who did you share your faith with this week and what were the results?

- The name Barnabas means "encourager." Whereas the Peter in our lives is busy encouraging us to take the next step in faith, the Barnabas in our lives is busy checking on our well-being, listening with compassionate ears, and not just offering words of wisdom but lifting us up in prayer as well. It is a wise and well-grounded church that facilitates the ministry of as many Barnabases as it can raise up. So, before you read the next paragraph, why not pick up the phone and call someone and ask how you can pray for them this week? Don't just be a "reader" of our words—be a doer too.

- Paul was Timothy's mentor—and though all of us need a Timothy, what's more important is there are many potential Timothys out there who need us. The fact is, no one becomes a spiritual giant without taking someone with them on the journey. It's a rule of leadership, and it's a rule of Christianity.

One of the keys to ensure the future of the church is to embrace the "Do no ministry alone" mantra. In other words, take your "Timothy" with you. There is virtually nothing church leaders do in the name of the church that's meant to be a lone-ranger task. If church leaders always took someone with them, there wouldn't be a leadership vacuum in the church today.

Even Dorothy realized fear is best conquered when you travel the Yellow Brick Road with companions. Regardless of the book, program, or package you use in your adult spiritual formation ministries, successfully taming the Hard-times Beast of fear takes faithful companions on the journey. This is not an area to cut; it's an area to emphasize.

In the best of times, the church is filled with potential Timothys. But when times get hard, more folks are willing to travel the faith-development path than at any other time.

Accountability Question: How would you rate the fear factor of yourself, your church, and the leaders?

YOUR LEADERS' RESPONSE TO FEAR IS CRITICAL

Just after 9/11, when our country's alert status went up to the highest it can go, my (BE) e-mail box overflowed from leaders seeking direction on what to say to their congregations. Here was my response.

- Be calm and remind them that nothing can separate them from the love of God.
- Be calm and fill them with many of the ways God has been with you in your times of trial.
- Be calm and share with them some of the promises God has made to those who believe.
- Be calm and help them see that courage, not fear, is the legacy of faith in Jesus Christ.
- Be calm and remind them, as James says, we can learn to count it all joy when surrounded by all kinds of trials.
- Be calm and demonstrate contempt for fear.
- Be calm and pray for the fearful that they might find faith.
- Be calm and show them the airline ticket you just purchased, or tell them that you are going to sleep with the windows open, or that you're planning a trip overseas, or whatever might lend some humor to the moment.

I signed the e-mail, "from Bill Easum, calm, cool, and, collected—firmly holding my out-of-the-country airline ticket in my white-knuckled hand."

MOVING ON

Before leaving this chapter, remember the promise: "Perfect love casts out all fear." What we're asking you to do during the remainder of this book is to put your fear aside and focus on the mission God has given all of us—to "make disciples of all nations"(Matthew 28:18). And remember, with God all things are possible. So let's proceed.

SUGGESTED READING

Growing Spiritual Redwoods, by Bill Easum and Tom Bandy. Abingdon (1997), 215 pp.

High-Voltage Spirituality, by Bill Tenny-Brittian. Chalice Press (2006), 192 pp.

Leading on Empty, by Wayne Cordeiro. Bethany House (2009), 224 pp.

Note

1. Bill Tenny-Brittian, *High Voltage Spirituality* (St. Louis: Chalice Press, 2006).

SEVEN

BUDGET ITEMS YOU ALWAYS INCREASE IN HARD TIMES

Worship and Children's Ministry

If you've followed our advice in chapter 5, you've freed up some money to spend on the ministries that will help you thrive during hard times. This chapter shows you the first places to spend that money as fast as you can.

The Hard Times Budget Formula

Always Increase:

Worship
Children's Ministry
Evangelism
Marketing
Continuing Education
Volunteer Ministries
Small Groups
Spiritual Formation

Some ministries are so important to a church that no matter what type of economy a church finds itself in they shouldn't be cut. We were extra careful and stingy compiling this list because we felt the longer we made the list the less strategic it would be. Items that appear on this list are crucial to the future of *any* church at *any* time, but in hard times the more time, energy, and money you can pour into them, the more likely your church is to remain strong.

WORSHIP

The Sunday morning worship service continues to be the primary "front door" to the church for the unconnected. Ask any never-churched North American what day and time "church" is, and they'll say "Sunday morning." If a guest spontaneously makes it to your congregation unannounced and not personally invited by another member, they'll most likely "show up" sometime on Sunday morning, and if they couldn't find your website or didn't drive by to see your half-hidden sign with the service times on it, they'll show up around 11-ish. Worship is where most people decide if they are returning and where most people connect with the pastor. Never lose sight of the fact that two key ingredients of your future depend on the authenticity of your worship:

- The bulk of your money is given during worship;
- People return to your church for a second visit depending on what and who they experienced at worship.

> When times are tough and the culture is changing, worship is the key place a church needs to spend more time, energy, and money.

Yet most dying churches spend precious little time, energy, or money in this area. When times are tough and the culture is changing, worship is the key place a church needs to spend more time, energy, and money. Instead of cutting back on personnel, churches need to add worship personnel during hard times. We have long been an advocate for a worship leader being the second most important hire. We have also beaten the drum for almost three decades for indigenous, rather than traditional, worship. The boats no longer come from Europe laden with churchgoers, and yet far too many churches still cling to a European form of linear worship.

It just stands to reason when redirecting money that one of the prime targets should be worship. Here's what we mean by adequately funding your worship.

- You should allocate 25 to 30 percent of your total budget for worship. This amount includes staff, music, musicians, set design, and digital media (audio and visual). Don't be afraid of paying some of your musicians, especially the one or two who really create the atmosphere.

Accountability Question: Is 25 percent or more of your budget going into worship?

- You have the equivalent of a full-time worship leader who is responsible for the overall worship experience each week. This is the most important person on the staff next to the pastor, and most dying churches do not have this position. Instead they have a part-time choir director whose sole responsibility is to get the choir ready to sing in worship. This person does little, if anything, to expand the number of people in the choir or increase their spiritual life. If the truth were known, many choir directors wouldn't be caught dead in a church if they weren't getting paid to direct the choir and weren't allowed to hire out to give music lessons.

Take a look in the appendix at the job description for a worship leader, and you will see how different this position is from a music director. This person makes sure the teams are in place to make the experience memorable and also is responsible for being their spiritual shepherd. It's much more than waving their hands in time with the beat.

Accountability Question: Do you have the equivalent of a full-time worship leader?

If 25 to 30 percent of your budget isn't devoted to worship and you don't have the equivalent of a full-time worship leader, you need to do whatever it takes to redirect as much money as you can to achieving these two goals as soon as you can.

As goes the worship, so goes the church, especially in hard times. So it amazes us that so many churches still insist on putting on their most "classic," "traditional," or "old-fashioned" worship service at a prime time on Sunday morning (prime time is either 10:00 or 11:00 a.m.). The problem is, when a guest drops into this service, it's likely to be the most irrelevant offering the church has. This is especially true if the guest is a member of the fast-growing "never-been-to-church" crowd. The question we pose to you is this: How likely do you suppose it is that someone who doesn't understand the liturgy, is unacquainted with the traditional customs, and is clueless about the language, will manage to walk away inspired and fulfilled from this service? Yes, stranger things have happened and the Holy Spirit will do what the Holy Spirit will do, but in the real world, there are but a handful of people who will fit into the exception category. Most will leave the service and never return, regardless of how friendly and hospitable you are. In hard times, you can't afford the luxury of parochialism or irrelevance.

But traditional worship services aren't the only form of worship that is uninspiring in our churches today. Any worship service that isn't life-informing and life-transforming will drive all but the most congregationally committed members from your church. Music that is anachronistic and sermons that are simplistic, boring, or immaterial to living life in these hard times simply have no place in the church today. They won't work in good times, much less in hard times.

We've found, after years of conversations with church members of declining churches, that one of the chief reasons they won't invite their friends, relatives, acquaintances, neighbors, co-workers, or anyone else is because they're painfully aware that their church offers *them* very little relevance, let alone offering help to the unconnected seeking a touch from God.

One of the confessions I've (BTB) had to make over the years is that there have been times in my life as a pastor and as a layperson that I refused to invite, let alone bring, a guest to my church. I've learned the hard way that with an unchurched person I only get one chance. If I take them to a church worship service that is uninspiring, they are unlikely to return.

But here's the clincher for me. Not only are they unlikely to return to *my* church, they're unlikely to return to any church.

There is never a good time for an uninspiring worship service, but in hard times there's simply no room for it.

PRACTICAL, ENCOURAGING MESSAGES THAT INSTILL HOPE

Often pastors fall into the same trap as the media—they fill their message with a veneer of fear that shakes the congregation to the core. Although their intentions may be good and they may be offering some excellent advice, the underlying message reinforces the Hard-times Beast. In hard times, every topic, phrase, and word must carry both hope and assurance.

> In hard times, every topic, phrase, and word must carry both hope and assurance.

For many Christians the worship service is a pivotal moment in their week. During the worship service you may well have your best opportunity to touch a heart and reach a soul. But that won't happen in hard times if you find yourself sucked into the quagmire of hand-wringing and worry-warting. In hard times, Christians and non-Christians alike make their way to the church building with a dim glimmer of hope. Even if it's barely a glimmer, and you can be sure it's there, the last thing these seekers want or need to be reminded of is how terrible things are. They already saw the news. And yet time and again we hear preachers standing in pulpits declaring a state of emergency on behalf of the church.

The reality is you shouldn't talk excessively about finances. On the other hand, one of the reasons we're in this mess is that there have been precious few speaking forthrightly and honestly about a Christian's financial responsibility. But what you say in the pulpit *must* carry hope and assurance. It's not about wearing rose-colored glasses but about leaving room for Jesus in all this.

You're probably familiar with Abraham Maslow. In 1943 he proposed his "Hierarchy of Needs" pyramid that has been the foundation for much of contemporary psychology and sociology ever since (see illustration below). In hard times, the church needs to be particularly aware of this pyramid.

MASLOW'S HIERARCHY OF NEEDS

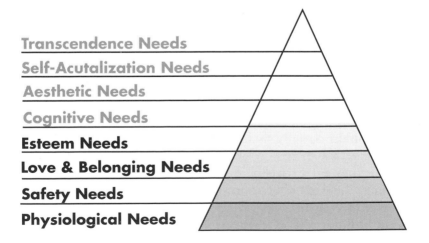

Transcendence Needs
Self-Acutalization Needs
Aesthetic Needs
Cognitive Needs
Esteem Needs
Love & Belonging Needs
Safety Needs
Physiological Needs

Level 1 Needs: Physiological—Breathing, Food, Water, Sleep, Sex, Homeostasis, Excretion

Level 2 Needs: Safety—Security of Body, Employment, Resources, Morality, Family, Health, Property

Level 3 Needs: Love/Belonging—Friendship, Family, Intimacy, Being Accepted

Level 4 Needs: Esteem—Self-Esteem, Confidence, Achievement, Recognition, Respect

Level 5.1 Needs: Cognitive—Knowledge, Understanding, Problem-Solving, Exploration

Level 5.2 Needs: Aesthetic—Symmetry, Order, Beauty

Level 5.3 Needs: Self-Actualization—Self-Fulfillment, Self-Efficacy, Creativity, Spontaneity

Level 5.4 Needs: Transcendence—Altruism, Service, Wonder, Beyond Ego, Contribution, Connection, Wholeness

Take a good look at these basic needs, especially the foundational tiers. It's easy to see how hard times are a challenge to most people. These basic needs are the ones most affected by hard times. Four of the eight basic needs of humanity are negatively affected by hard times. That means during hard times your people are suffering, not just in the pocketbook, but in most areas of their lives.

> During hard times your people are suffering, not just in the pocketbook, but in most areas of their lives.

With that in mind, you can see how preaching a good, solid, theological treatise that appeals to the cognitive needs, including problem-solving, is likely to miss the target completely, especially when fear is the predominant emotion floating through the congregation's spirit. Instead, effective preaching in hard times must focus on the simplicity of the gospel and help people return to the foundation of the faith with encouraging words. This doesn't mean sermons should be fluff or culturally popular—far from it. In times like these, you're going to have to return to the basics of commitment, forgiveness, and integrity. John reminds us that "perfect love drives out fear" (1 John 4:18 NIV). Your challenge in your preaching is to inspire your congregation to perfection in love.

WHAT PEOPLE NEED FROM YOUR PREACHING

In times like these, when the culture is changing and the economic picture is spiraling down the tubes, people need an anchor on which to cling to keep themselves afloat. Here are some thoughts about the kind of anchors needed in today's preaching.

- People need certainty in a world based on uncertainty. They need to know Jesus is the same yesterday, today, and forever. They need to know that the historical Jesus and the Christ of faith are one and the same. The need for certainty is one of the reasons liberal, mainline Protestantism is in such serious decline—they find it hard to be certain about Jesus and eternal life. It is also one of the reasons we don't feel the Emergent Movement is going to be as much of a major player in the emerging world as some people think. The Emergent people are passionate but seldom certain. That won't play well in a wildcard world, with the exception of the Christian intelligentsia—and that's a rapidly shrinking audience. "Therefore let all the house of Israel know for certain that God has made Him both Lord and Christ—this Jesus whom you crucified" (Acts 2:36 NASB).
- People need direction in a world that's being torn apart. The need for direction is the primary reason we don't think effective churches can be run by consensus. A wildcard world doesn't wait for people to form consensus (yes, we know there are a variety of ways to define consensus, but all of them take time that churches don't have in hard times). If churches are to survive in this emerging world, they need leaders who aren't afraid to set the agenda and give direction to the church.

This isn't a popular stance to take. There is much comfort in a majority-ruled church. Everyone gets heard. Everyone has a say. But there is simply too much at stake and changes are happening too fast for consensus-building. It's especially critical in hard times for leaders to lead with certainty, confidence, and direction.

- People need hope in a world that is basically broken. Very little in the United States is working these days. Every day the news shares some story about the brokenness of our society. Churches that offer a healthy dose of hope have a much greater chance of growing than do those who are always pointing fingers at the sinners.

Take a good look at how Jesus handled sinners. The only finger-wagging he did was at the good "religious" folk (including his own disciples). To the crowds, he offered hope and a better way—and he offered it without bad-mouthing their current situation. Look back over your last six months of messages and see how many were filled with hope. The more they are, the more likely your people and your church are to grow.

We need to be careful here. By hope, we're not talking about a Pollyanna approach to life. Hope has to be grounded in Scripture, not in psychology. Hope has to be real, not saccharine. Ground the hope you offer in the Jesus who is the same yesterday, today, and forever. "For we through the Spirit, by faith, are waiting for the hope of righteousness" (Galatians 5:5 NASB).

WHAT YOU NEED TO TELL YOUR PEOPLE

We are moving from a consumer-oriented, overextended, immediate gratification world to a buyer's market, bankruptcy, and delayed gratification world. Most people under forty have never known anything but the consumer type of world. That world is being turned upside down and many won't know how to cope with the world that's emerging.

Therefore, your preaching should have two goals. The first is to address the spiritual issues they are facing, and the second is to offer practical tips for surviving in this new world. Here are some practical things they need to hear.

- Don't max out your credit cards. In fact one card is better than two. And no card is better than one. Learn to live within your means and pay off your credit card every month.
- Don't take out a second mortgage on your home no matter how bad it gets.
- If you don't have a fixed rate mortgage, get one.
- If you're retired, don't use more than 3 percent of your savings per year unless you are a multi-millionaire.

CHILDREN'S MINISTRY

Children's ministry continues to be one of the two key ministries in growing churches. In many growing churches, children constitute one-half or more of the people on Sunday. A children's ministry is often one of the key side doors to the church.

Unlike youth, children are not as able to fend for themselves or to raise their own funds. They also require significant adult supervision. Parents are much more concerned about the safety of young children than they are that of older youth. Keep in mind that part of our focus on children's ministry is getting the parents to return for a second visit. How well you care for their children will be more important to that decision than what you have for their youth. So the children's ministry is not a place to save money. It's a place to spend extra money during hard times. Parents have enough worries without adding one more to their list because your children's area is not safe or does not look well kept.

Parents often return to a church based on their children's response to Sunday morning. It is not unusual upon leaving Sunday morning for parents to ask their children what they did during Sunday school or children's church. Their response is crucial to whether that family will return for another visit.

So spend a few dollars sprucing up the children's area. It's amazing what some fresh paint can do to an area. If you have any artists in the church, ask them to paint a mural in the hallway leading into the children's area. Happy kid equals happy parents.

During hard times, fear rises to the surface even if it isn't warranted. So the last thing parents need is to worry about leaving their child in what appears to be an unsafe environment. Notice we said "in what appears to be." You would do well to ask an unchurched friend who is a parent to take a look at your children's area, including the nursery, and tell you if it appears to be safe and clean.

Children's ministries have undergone major change over the last two decades. The changing family structures mean that parents take less responsibility for their children and their spiritual development. The number of children with emotional and physical special needs is skyrocketing due to neglect and fetal drug and alcohol syndrome. The church also must compete with community activities such as sports and video games.

> In good times or bad times, nothing is as important to the growth of a church as the power of worship and the care of children.

Another major change is the increasing legal implications of children's ministry. It's imperative that your children's workers, both paid and volunteer, be screened for abuse charges and even allegations. Then there are the safety issues. Make sure you're in compliance with local, state, and federal laws. Security and litigation are increasingly important and consuming more time on the part of the children's ministry.

Children's education has changed from children quietly sitting in a semicircle around a flannel board listening to a teacher tell a story. Today's effective Christian education embraces interactive and participatory learning with an increasing awareness of the many ways children learn today. In the current culture, life-changing learning seldom takes place at a desk.

The smaller the numbers of children who attend your church, the more attention you have to pay to what we call "critical mass." Critical mass refers to the number of children in a group. When there are fewer than five children in a room, it can be painfully intimidating for a new child. If your classes don't have critical mass, you would do well to move away from the classroom model to a model where the elementary children are grouped together to form a larger group. If you have enough children to put first through third graders together and fourth through fifth together, do so. Offer them contemporary children's music, videos, and a great storyteller. Then break them into smaller groups to see what they've learned.[1]

MOVING ON

In good times or bad times, nothing is as important to the growth of a church as the power of worship and the care of children. Make sure you put as much time, energy, and *money* into these two areas as you possibly can.

SUGGESTED READING

Postmodern Children's Ministry, by Ivy Beckwith. Zondervan (2004), 176 pp.

Preaching: The Art of Narrative Exposition, by Calvin Miller. Baker Books (2006), 288 pp.

Unfreezing Moves, by Bill Easum. Abingdon (2002), 176 pp.

Worship Evangelism, by Sally Morgenthaler. Zondervan (1999), 320 pp.

Note

1. See *Promise Land* from Willow Creek, or *Up Street* from North Pointe in Atlanta.

EIGHT

BUDGET ITEMS YOU ALWAYS INCREASE IN HARD TIMES

Evangelism and Marketing

The hunker-down-in-the-bunker mentality will kill your church. It will cause your congregation to turn inward and focus on survival. As your leaders focus inward, the "What's in it for me?" attitude takes over and the call to make disciples is lost. When that happens, the church ceases being the church of Jesus Christ and becomes a club or hospice or hospital. The only way back to being a church is for your leaders to take the focus off survival and "me" and notice the lost masses that surround the church every day.

The Hard Times Budget Formula
Always Increase:

Worship
Children's Ministry
Evangelism
Marketing
Continuing Education
Volunteer Ministries
Small Groups
Spiritual Formation

EVANGELISM

In tough economic times, churches that thrive will be those that equip their members to connect with their unchurched friends who are struggling and offer them relevant hope and a compelling invitation. Some examples might be equipping your members to invite their unchurched friends to: a new Bible study on Ezekiel or 2 Timothy; a message series entitled "How to Survive in Tough Times"; or an offering of Dave Ramsey's Financial Peace University.[1]

Key participants in the church need to understand that their everyday work and play are avenues for sharing their faith and their church. They need to be encouraged to develop networks of unconnected people much like is done on websites such as FaceBook. And then intentionally work those relationships on behalf of the kingdom of God.

Accountability Question: Pastor, how often do you encourage your people to share their faith? How often do you share your faith outside of the pulpit? How often do you make evangelism training events possible? How often do you provide fishing pools in which your leaders can fish? That's why our group, 21st Century Strategies (formerly Easum, Bandy & Associates), conducts seminars around the country on how to share your faith.

FINDING THE KEY TO THE CITY

Every community has a key that unlocks the city to evangelism. Discovering that key is essential. I've (BE) had three churches in my lifetime and all three had different keys: one was shearing sheep with ranchers; one was playing shuffleboard with senior citizens; and the last one was spending time at a favorite watering hole with prostitutes and alcoholics.

Accountability Question: Pastor, what's the key to your city? Have you spent time trying to locate it?

Pastors, as well as the congregation, need to be connecting with unconnected people. And here is some good news—in hard times people will be more open to the gospel than during good times. They will be more eager to hear how God made a difference in your life and could do so in their life. During hard times, people are far more ready to attend church or to listen to what Christians have to say about living life. So this is a time to redirect as much time, energy, and money as you can to reaching out to your community with the good news.

THE METHODS ARE CHANGING AND HARD TIMES WILL PLAY TO THE CHANGE

Prior to the 1960s, pastors impersonally "preached" people into the kingdom and people "walked the aisles for Jesus." Local churches held revivals targeting non-Christians. With little or no prior relationship, people were encouraged to give their lives to Jesus on the spot—and they did. Denominational headquarters turned out canned "programs" geared to preparing church members to be evangelists. People were taught how to use Evangelism Explosion or to lead people through the Four Spiritual Laws. As effective as these methods were, they started losing their effectiveness the closer we got to the twenty-first century. Churches that hold onto these outdated methods will find fewer and fewer people "walking the aisle."

> In the emerging world, effective evangelism relies on long-term relationships and growth processes, not rallies, laws, or programs.

The modern world took a cognitive approach to discipleship, beginning with belief, moving to belonging, and resulting in behaving. Today's experiential culture requires just the opposite. Discipleship moves from becoming part of a community of friends, to changing one's behavior, to belief in the God seen and shared in those new friends' lives.

73

Many of the conversions recorded in the twentieth century were dramatic, immediate, "Damascus-road" experiences. My (BE) own conversion occurred that way. One day a drifting, rebellious, alcoholic teenager, the next day I was literally preaching the gospel. However, the gradual, looking-back, Emmaus experience gives us a better way of describing conversion today. As recounted in Luke 24, Jesus joined two men on the road to Emmaus. Along the way they had a conversation. Later they realized they had been with Jesus.

It is not unusual for individuals to take two to four years to realize that they have committed their lives to God through Christ. Did you get that? It can take two to four years *to realize that they have committed* their lives to God through Christ. Identifying the moment of "conversion" is a rare occurrence today.

Several years ago, my (BE) worship team and I did a short workshop tour. At one stop our drummer got sick and we needed a replacement. The only replacement we could find, a non-Christian, rehearsed with the group each evening before the workshops. On the third evening he said to the group, "This has been an awesome experience. I don't know what you folks have, but I want it. I don't think I'll ever be the same again. Tell me more about Jesus." I don't know what happened to this guy, but that night he took the first step on a journey of faith.

There's another way to describe what's going on. We're moving from "being saved" to "being transformed." Being transformed differs significantly from being saved. Being saved suggests an event, whereas being transformed suggests a long-term process through a variety of events. Involvement in the mission out of which one is transformed is often the end result of being transformed. It can be hard to separate one's transformation from one's mission. Behavior and belief are merging. For this reason, membership in a church no longer constitutes the goal. In many cases the only purpose for encouraging membership is to be able to hold key leaders to a higher standard of behavior than before.

What are the implications of this change and how are they affected by hard times?

- In the Western world, conversion takes longer and requires more people along the way. Whereas this can be a problem in a busy, mobile world, it will be easier in hard times. Believe it or not, in hard times some people have more leisure time and they're certainly not as mobile, so there will be time to invest in these long-term relationships.
- We must view evangelism as a systematic process rather than a program that needs a committee. An evangelism committee suggests that evangelism is a particular program or ministry handled by just a few. Instead, evangelism must become the mission of everyone, not just a committee. The church must retool everything it does so that it is evangelistic. Every program and every disciple takes part in the process. The way each disciple lives and relates to those around him or her affects the process. Christians must understand the importance of working together in evangelism. This shift is helpful during hard times because churches don't have to purchase a program to practice evangelism.
- Instead of evangelism as a mostly "one-to-one" experience, it appears to be moving more toward a group process (like our drummer experienced). Paul's formula in 1 Corinthians 3:6 presents a good way to look at evangelism at the turn of this century: "I planted, Apollos watered, but God gave the growth" (NRSV). For this reason we continue to stress the importance of small groups that form around behavior modification, much like the Wesley Class Meeting. And, as we've said before, small groups meeting in homes don't cost the church anything except for the hard work of training, mentoring, and coaching the leaders.
- People respond better to groups or individuals with the same life-experiences they have had (e.g., alcoholic

to recovering alcoholic or non-Christian to someone who did not grow up in the church). We all come from specific contexts and backgrounds. The fact is no one individual can reach everyone. Therefore, churches should consider forming "contextual pools" from which to bring together people with similar backgrounds. A contextual pool could have a list of all the committed disciples in the fellowship, along with their backgrounds and gifts. A disciple who encounters an alcoholic in need of God could then dip into the contextual pool and draw out the name of a Christian friend who is a recovering alcoholic or a small group of recovering alcoholics and connect them in some relational way with the person in need. We don't mention alcoholics lightly. We mention them prominently because hard times always significantly increase alcoholism and other addictions.

The further we move into the twenty-first century, the more important the relational, affirmational, contextual, and group evangelism will become. Just as the days of the charismatic, "Bible-thumping" evangelists are over, so are the days of the programmatic evangelism committee. In their place the church will have to be the church once again: people on a mission to teach and baptize all nations in the name of Jesus Christ.

MARKETING

I (BTB) was called in to do a worship training event at a church. The church wasn't growing, even though the town around it was. I soon discovered two huge reasons the church wasn't growing. The first had to do with visibility—or invisibility as the case may be. The church had an excellent location and the building was highly visible. It even had a pretty good reputation among those few who knew of the church. But even though the church sat on Main Street, almost no one other than the members knew it was there. The second problem was that when a guest *did* manage to wander into the church, they were greeted by a general inhospitality. The church wasn't ugly to visitors; it just basically ignored them.

In hard times, your church can't afford to waste any opportunity that walks through the door. And it can't afford to not maximize its reputation and known presence in the community. This section will briefly look at both of these issues and offer suggestions as to:

- How you can get your congregation looking outward;
- How to create some opportunities to get the unconnected connecting to both Jesus and your congregation.

THE "M" WORD

It wasn't that many years ago when I (BTB) was working with a transforming congregation that I let the "M" word slip out between my teeth. The moment I mentioned the word *marketing* the chair of the board got tight-jawed and said, "The gospel isn't for sale." Marketing was a "secular" word that apparently couldn't be mentioned on holy ground—or even in a board meeting.

Regardless of your view on the word *marketing*, the fact is if the unconnected don't know who you are and what you're about, when hard times (and the Spirit) bring them to a place where they're willing to overcome their prejudices or bad experiences with organized religion in order to walk through a church's doors, it won't be your doors they're walking through. It will be the one down the street that wasn't there ten years ago and is now ten times the size of your church because they go out of their way to welcome the stranger.

The best definition of marketing we've ever heard is a simple three-word phrase—marketing is "to make friends." The Scriptures call marketing "taking the bushel off the light" (see Luke 11:33). Call it what you want, if you and your congregation make enough friends, your congregation's going to score opportunities.

There are three broad areas of marketing we're going to briefly explore: mass marketing, presence marketing, and word-of-mouth marketing.

MASS MARKETING

Mass marketing is what most of us think about when we hear the "M" word. Churches regularly spend money on Yellow Pages ads and newspaper ads. Open your phone book, if you're old enough to still have one, and look through the church ads. Any space that's larger than even a quarter-page is a major investment. We used to recommend churches invest in an ad in the phone book. We seldom suggest that anymore unless your target audience is the fifty-plus crowd. Younger folks seldom consult paper, choosing instead to let their fingers do their searching in the Google pages.

However, if you're going to continue to put an ad in the phone book, you'll need to make a couple of choices. In most metropolitan areas, you'll have to decide in which phone book you want your ad. Once you've decided which Yellow Book, you have to

Fragmentation of Mass Marketing

In the 1950s an episode of *I Love Lucy* drew 70 percent of available audience. Today, *Desperate Housewives* draws less than a third of *Lucy's* ratings.

Today more people watch cable TV than are watching the three major networks.

In 1993 there were 130 websites; today there are tens of millions.

In 2001 there were virtually zero blogs; today there are over 30 million and exploding by the second.

In the 1960s an advertiser could reach 80 percent of U.S. women airing an evening commercial simultaneously on the three major networks; today it would take more than 100 TV channels to reach the same audience.

Niche media is growing: Cable TV, podcasting, wireless messaging, the Internet, and Google ads.

decide how much to spend. We recommend not investing much beyond the cost of getting a bold heading and perhaps including the times of your weekend worship services. Of course, if you do that, you're locked in for at least a year.

During hard times newspapers are hard hit. Right now major newspapers across the country are filing for bankruptcy and cutting back to two or three issues a week. True, these cutbacks have been coming for a long time, but they are increasing exponentially now. On top of the economic crunch, except in rural small towns, newspaper circulation is largely limited to older adults who have the time and take comfort in the feel of real paper. The implication of this cutback is huge for the church. If your church hopes to reach the under-forty crowd, spending money on newspaper advertising is an expensive enterprise for the return. If you're going to run newsprint advertising, limit it to Christmas and Easter week.

However, so long as your newspaper is doing business, it will still be reporting news—at least somewhere between all those ads. If your congregation is doing something newsworthy (a rummage sale or bean soup supper is not news), make sure your local paper knows about it. Learn to write an effective news release, and if the paper runs the story, you'll also keep the seniors apprised of what's going on.

Where *should* you spend money in mass marketing? The first place is with your church signage. Yes, if you do it right, your sign can be one tool in your mass marketing toolkit. I (BTB) recently visited a church located on a busy city street and noticed their church sign was flush with the building and was less than four feet by three feet. No one could see the sign. Make sure yours can be seen.

One more note about your church sign. If you have a message board sign, do not use it for Internet pithy sayings. Can you imagine McDonalds using their sign to say "Hamb-rger. The Only Thing Missing Is U"? Cute sayings don't bring new people into your church. Use your sign for what it was designed for—to let people know what's going on in the church that might appeal to them. If you have a great sermon series coming up, make sure people know about it. But make sure the title of the series isn't in code or so obscure that the average unconnected passerby doesn't "get it." A sermon series called "Making It Through Tough Times" is more likely to attract a guest than "Wisdom Tales."

PRESENCE MARKETING

A time once existed when a newly constructed church could hang out a sign that pronounced its "brand" and people would show up. The "build it and they will come" days are basically at an end. However, there are three exceptions to the "build it and they will come" rule, especially in hard times.

Your Web Presence

When it comes to marketing, if you build a website and put it where those looking for you expect it, they will visit the site.

In today's culture it still shocks us to discover how many churches have either no website or an inadequate website. According to a number of sources today, nearly 85 percent of people considering going to church begin on the Internet. *If* they find your site, they'll look at the content of the home page and at most one or two other pages before they decide whether they are going to visit. This means you need to build a website primarily based on unconnected people rather than on your members' expectations and convenience.

Your website should have a memorable Universal Resource Locator (URL), otherwise known as your domain name. Many Internet users will guess at a URL and type it into the address bar to see what they get. Indeed, the new Google Chrome Internet browser currently doesn't even have a separate search bar—you type in your best guess for the site you're looking for in the address bar and it tries to match it to the domain name first and as a search term second. So, if you live in Lee Summit, you might consider a domain name like www.firstchurchleesummit.com. It may seem a bit long, but it's memorable, logical, and is infinitely better than a string of seemingly unrelated letters such as www.jcmoabc.org (Jefferson City, Missouri, American Baptist Church).

On your home page, visitors should see your worship service times and a prominent directions button or link, if not the address itself (preferably linked to an online map). And please avoid the edifice complex that seems to plague most churches. Pictures of people score way better than pictures of your church building.

Your New Church or Multi-site Service

It seems the converse may be true when it comes to build it and they will come. If you build a church (or start a multi-site service) where everyone expects it to be, it's unlikely that it will get noticed. However, put a new church or a new service where no one expects it (of course, it must also be visible) and you're likely to draw some curiosity seekers on a regular basis. Some churches are buying old Wal-Mart buildings and converting them with good success. Others are purchasing malls or space inside a mall with good results (storefront churches in strip malls aren't novel enough). The key is to get noticed so you can make new friends.

WOMM

The phrase "What's the buzz?" is taking on more meaning in hard times. Let us explain.

The buzz is Word of Mouth Marketing (WOMM). It is still true today that the majority of participants in a church initially attend because they were invited by a friend, relative, acquaintance, neighbor, or coworker.

> Word-of-mouth marketing is replacing many of the standard marketing practices—and it's free.

In the book *Applebee's America: How Successful Political, Business and Religious Leaders Connect with the New American Community*, the authors suggest we are moving back into a pre-TV world where word of mouth is going to be the major form of spreading one's message or selling a product. Already more and more major companies are shifting their advertising dollars from traditional media to niche and word-of-mouth media. According to the authors, one of the challenges for organizations is to adjust to this new reality and to learn the word-of-mouth rules. *We shouldn't have to remind you that word-of-mouth marketing is free.*

Those of you who know us know we have long been proponents of television and direct mail marketing. While we are still proponents of these two media, we too have become less convinced of their effectiveness.

In the past, organizations could count on using the traditional media, such as radio, television, and direct mail to reach a large percentage of the public. Today, none of these are as reliable as they once were. Now, *word of mouth* is taking their place.

The first axiom of WOMM is that church folk will actively invite their friends *only* if there's something worth inviting them to. In hard times, the church ought to be a beacon of hope and assurance. However, if church members don't experience hope and assurance, you can bet they're not going to be inviting their unconnected friends. If they don't see lives being transformed, they're not going to believe their friends are going to be transformed either.

The second axiom of WOMM is that the best "sales aid" is a satisfied customer. Rick Warren has largely built the Saddleback Church on this principle. Every week he has someone on the stage sharing how their life has been dramatically transformed by a Saddleback ministry. Imagine what your church might be like if you had fifty-two people every year sharing how God had changed their lives through the ministries at your church. It won't happen overnight, but over the long haul—and even in the short haul—people will start talking. And when they share with a neighbor, it's called WOMM.

The third axiom of WOMM is that there is a group of people in every organization who have unusual connections in the community. Oprah Winfrey is an example of one of these people. Here is a sample list of some of the people who normally have the potential of having an unusual number of contacts in the community.

- Pastors who speak on Sunday
- Small group leaders
- Children and youth directors
- Realtors
- Stay-at-home moms who carpool
- People who e-mail a lot
- Politicians
- Children's league coaches
- Influential people in business
- Bus drivers
- Taxi cab drivers
- Consultants
- Authors

Who would you add to the list?

Most people can be trained to be more successful in connecting with people. Here are some ways to train your people to connect better with people and keep the buzz going.

- Make and maintain a "gut values" connection with people. By that we mean be sure whatever you do offers people a sense of community, authenticity, and higher purpose. This must begin in the worship service and extend out into all of the ministries. For example: Rick Warren sent a letter to prospective people in the community that did not mention God or Christ. Instead his letter appealed to gut values: "Meet new friends and get to know your neighbors."
- Adapt to the social and demographic changes around you in ways that allow you to feel what people outside the church are feeling (of course never lower your standards or water down the gospel). Too many church leaders still function as if it were 1950, relying on old technologies,

methods, dress, and style of preaching. We have often commented that if the 1950s ever return, most churches will be ready. Please don't be one of them. Make sure your services are relevant to your community.

- Analyze and target groups in your community using lifestyle demographics (psychographics). In other words, you need to talk about the right things to the right group of people. When Wayne Cordeiro planted New Hope in Honolulu, he knew that family and food were inherent in the Hawaiian culture, so he centered his connections on those two things. He asked the members of his church in Hilo to write all of their family members in Honolulu and introduce Wayne to them. When he arrived in Honolulu, he simply invited those family members to a luau and the rest is history.

- Find the "connectors" in your church. Who are the people in your church who are most likely to invite their networks? These are your most valuable assets. Spend time identifying them and encouraging them to work their networks. Questions to ask are: Who are their friends? Where do they get their information? Who do they turn to for advice? What are their hobbies? What magazines do they read? Where do they live? What kind of car do they drive? What and how do they shop? What do they do for vacation? What angers them? What makes them happy? What do they do for a living? And what sport do they play? Once you have these questions answered, you know where to look for these folks and how to spot them. It will also help you be more relevant in your preaching and in your other ministries.

- Use multiple channels of communication to deliver relevant and timely messages. This is where the lectionary loses its luster since it's seldom timely to current events.

The following is a list of some of the key WOMM rules.
- Train every leader to work their networks.

- Everyone is a potential connector with someone who needs God.
- Some people are more influential than others and are the backbone of WOMM. Finding and training these people is crucial.
- Outgoing people are your church's best assets.
- Being relevant is crucial.
- Small groups are at the heart of most church WOMM campaigns.
- All conversation has to be honest.
- You have to deliver what you promise.
- Whatever you do must be so "gut-filling" and value-driven that people will tell their connections about it.
- Identifying, targeting, and equipping the connectors in your church is the role of all church staff.

MORE THAN MARKETING

Marketing is all well and good, but what happens when a guest actually shows up? What kind of welcome will they get? Every church thinks it's one of the friendliest in town, but there's a little secret that no one wants to tell you. In the world of the unconnected, *there's no such thing as a friendly church*. Oh sure, some are less hostile than others. And yes, we know, hostile is a strong word, but when it comes to a guest entering a foreign environment, there are only a few degrees between discomfort and terror.

> Hospitality begins in the parking lot.

There is ample evidence and research that claims visitors make up their mind about whether they are likely to return within two or three minutes from the time they park their car. Of course, children's programming and the worship quality and style have a lot to do with it as well; even so, it's better to not take any chances. You need to roll out the welcome mat as quickly as possible. The clock is ticking.

We've been reminding churches for decades that hospitality begins in the parking lot. And yet we've noticed that very few churches actually get the message and deploy parking lot greeters. For us, this is a no-brainer, and yet churches seem highly resistant to both the suggestion and the reality that the visitor's impression clock begins to run even before the key leaves the ignition.

I (BTB) was leading a Complete Worship Audit recently and noted that the church had two prominent signs to direct guests. Next to door number one, a welcome sign said "Sanctuary." Next to door number two, on the other side of the parking lot, a second welcome sign said "Worship Center." If you were an unconnected guest looking to visit a worship service and you had no church experience, which of the two buildings do you imagine you might walk toward? Of course, if the church had parking lot greeters, this wouldn't be an issue. They would greet guests, help them with their belongings if needed, and direct them to the correct entrance.

There are probably a hundred different hospitality tips we could offer here, but that's not the purpose of this book. There are a number of books on the subject and both of us have written extensively on hospitality on our blogs, in articles on our website, and in our books. But if you want to really find out where you're failing in the hospitality department, find yourself someone who's totally unconnected with Jesus and the church and pay them $50 to do a secret shopper visit during worship and get their honest, unbiased feedback. Of course, we offer the Complete Worship Audit[2] for congregations who want or need an assessment, specific recommendations, and training.

Just to get you started, though, we've included a brief bullet list of key hospitality issues.

- Do you have parking lot and outdoor greeters?
- Do your greeters greet gregariously?
- Do your ushers "ush," or do they just hand out bulletins?
- Can a guest easily find his or her way to the restrooms without having to ask anyone?

- Does your nursery get an A+ in the three S's? (Sanitation, Safety, and Security)
- Could a visitor wander off down an unmarked hallway and get lost? They can if there aren't visible signs in every corridor that point the direction to the worship space, the restrooms, and the nursery.
- Can a guest easily remain anonymous if they want to, or does your congregation risk embarrassing them by (1) identifying them with name badges that are different from member badges, or (2) publicly identifying them or introducing them during the worship service?
- Do your worship slides or bulletin use any "church" or "insider" language like invocation, Gloria Patri, CYF, UMW, BSF, Eucharist, intinction, "See Ann W.," benediction, and so on?
- Do you assume everyone "knows" the Lord's Prayer by heart?
- Do you risk discomforting your guests by holding hands or expecting physical contact, other than shaking hands in greeting?

A LESSON IN HOW TO BE HOSPITABLE TO STRANGERS

A couple of years ago I (BE) attended a workshop on "Managing Creativity" sponsored by Leadership Network and the Disney Institute in Orlando. The initial thought I had after less than two hours at Disney was, "Wouldn't it be exciting if our churches cared about welcoming strangers as much as Disney does?" Every Disney employee I met welcomed me as if they really were glad to see me.

Accountability Question: What if every person in your church was trained to welcome "angels unaware" when they pop in at your church? What if every person who visits your church left knowing that the people were glad they were there? Would it change the way your church achieves its mission?

After a few hours, it was apparent that everyone who works at Disney knows the Disney story—how it got started, what

Walt dreamed of creating, and what role they play in creating the Disney drama each day. Every person understood that they were a cast member of a giant play.

Accountability Question: What would change in your church if every leader understood that they were a cast member in the great drama of divine intervention into this world? Would it change the way your leaders came to church and responded to the guests? Consider how it would change the stranger's view of your church if every person they asked "What is this church all about?" was able to give them the same response.

It was also soon apparent that Disney had a code of conduct such as not smoking or chewing gum on the premises, saying Good Morning, Good Evening, Good Afternoon instead of Hello, or upon seeing someone taking a picture of their family, asking if they could take it for them so the family member could be in the picture. Simple things, but these things showed that the people of Disney were prepared to make anyone's trip to Disney an experience they would not forget.

Accountability Question: What if our church leaders were prepared to make each Sunday morning an unforgettable experience? What would you have to change to make that happen?

Disney demonstrates that the experience begins in the parking lot. All along the pathway from the parking lot to the entrance, speakers played Disney music, helping guests get in the mood. The parking lot was immaculate. Everything played to a theme. The landscaping was incredible.

Accountability Question: What does your parking lot or the absence thereof say to the stranger? Does it give the appearance that someone lives there? How about those weeds growing in the front lawn or the grass that has not been cut in several weeks? Or the snow that you leave piled up all winter on the parking lot?

I walked away from my Disney experience quietly praying, "God, what will it take for your people to care as much about sharing Jesus with strangers as Disney cares about making a profit?"

IN-HOUSE MARKETING

Let's assume visitors are dropping into your worship services and that your hospitality is at least adequate. What's going to bring Gary and Geri Guest back? Although we're certain your sermons are stellar, your choir or worship team are tops in the town, and your children's programming is out of sight, that may not be enough to get them to return. Especially in hard times, it's not just a "nice" place that the unconnected either need or want. If they're going to invest their time with your congregation, they need to know two things: (1) they've been noticed and appreciated, and (2) there's something worth coming back for.

> A gracious host is a host to everyone, especially those with whom they're unacquainted.

Visitors need to be noticed and appreciated. However, in the hospitality section we warned you about publicly identifying visitors and now we're telling you to make sure they've been noticed and appreciated. How do you do that without calling attention to them somehow?

Unless you're an over-the-top extrovert who is in need of public attention, you likely feel pretty uncomfortable when you're at your favorite Mexican restaurant and someone tells the server that it's your birthday. There's something about having to wear a tourist's sombrero while the whole restaurant sings "Happy Birthday" that drives most people away from Casa El Grande Burrito during their birth month. On the other hand, if you patronize the restaurant and they patently ignored you, you'd be incensed. When it comes to guests in church, somewhere in between is the answer. Match good service (hospitality) with a warm welcome and you've got a winning combination.

"But how will we know who's a guest and who's not?" we're asked. Here's where training your members in basic hospitality is critical. The best way to ensure every guest is greeted and made to feel welcome is for every regular participant to be a gracious host.

A gracious host is a host to everyone, especially those he or she is unacquainted with. Gracious hosts never allow a stranger to be a stranger. Instead, they're interested in "getting to know" everyone. So, when they see someone they don't know, even if that someone may or may not be a regular participant, they make their way over to them and introduce themselves, saying, "I don't believe we've met. I'm Bill." And then gracious hosts listen and get to know whomever they've met, member or guest or staff. If they're well-trained hosts who have just met a first-time visitor, they will introduce them to the pastor or to a staff member or to a small group leader or to someone who might "connect" with the guest because of some affinity.

Being noticed must be accompanied by being offered something worth returning for if the visitor is to come back a second time. The most precious commodity we have is time. In hard times, people tend to get more discriminating in how they spend not just their money but also their time. If an unconnected person from your community is to consider spending time with your congregation, they're going to want to know there's something worth investing in. One excellent way to invite/entice a guest to return is to offer them something of value if they do.

We're not talking about offering a bribe here. What we're suggesting is that you let your guest know about upcoming events, sermon series, seminars, classes, workshops, and so forth that would be of *particular* interest to them. The point is not to overwhelm them with a laundry list of things to do but to extend a specific invitation to a particular offering that might resonate with their perceived needs or desires. We call this a "handoff."

Handoffs have two parts—the event and the invitation. The event you choose to "offer" should be tailored specifically for the targeted audience. Part of noticing and appreciating the guest includes discovering some of the person's needs or interests.

You don't have to pry into a person's history to know something about what might interest them. For instance, if you want to reach young families, a sermon series on parenting or a seminar on making relationships work ABC (after birthing children) might be enticing. If you're targeting Baby Boomers, then classes on making the most of retirement investments or what to do when your parents move in with you might be good offerings. In hard times it might be something like a crash course in what the Bible says about handling money.

The second part of a handoff is the invitation. If you're a pastor, you already know how little effect announcements made from the pulpit and notices in the bulletin have. If you want your guests to take note, to remember, and maybe even to attend your handoff event, your invitation is going to have to be both substantial and significant.

Here is a three-pronged approach to the invitation.

- If you have video technology in your worship space (and if you don't, your congregation isn't serious about reaching the unconnected), put a couple of your teenagers in charge of creating a YouTube-quality commercial for the event. Tell them you need it to be eye-catching, that it needs to include the significant details, and if it can be tastefully humorous, all the better. Make sure you screen it, and if it's suitable, use it in worship.
- Create a colorful flier or brochure on the event and insert it into the bulletin.
- And there's nothing like a personal invitation from someone who relates to the guest and who will be attending the event as well. This three-pronged approach offers you the best possibility for a response to your handoff.

MOVING ON

In hard times you must make opportunities and then make the most of the opportunities God gives you. Evangelism, marketing, hospitality, and handoffs will help your congregation do more than just survive in hard times. They'll help you thrive.

SUGGESTED READING

Applebee's America: How Successful Political, Business and Religious Leaders Connect with the New American Community, by Ron Fournier, et al. Simon and Schuster (2007), 260 pp.

Evangelism in the Early Church, by Michael Green. Eerdmans (2004), 474 pp.

The Hitchhiker's Guide to Evangelism, by Bill Tenny-Brittian. Chalice (2009), 167 pp.

The Influentials: One American in Ten Tells the Other Nine How to Vote, Where to Eat, and What to Buy, by Jon Berry and Ed Keller. Simon and Schuster (2003), 368 pp.

The Public Relations Writer's Handbook, by Merry Aronson, et al. Jossey-Bass (2007), 368 pp.

The Sticky Church, by Larry Osborne. Zondervan (2008), 208 pp.

Notes

1. Dave Ramsey, Financial Peace University at http://www.dave ramsey.com/fpu/home/

2. http://easumbandy.com/services/secret_shopping/

NINE

BUDGET ITEMS YOU ALWAYS INCREASE IN HARD TIMES

Continuing Education
and Volunteer Ministries

T he tougher the times, the more wisdom required of the church's key leaders. Leaders will have to learn how to do more with less and adjust on the fly. Trying just to keep a church's head above water always results in a loss of momentum—one of the deadly killers of good organizations during hard times. That's why we include continuing education in the "Always Increase" section of the Hard Times Budget. In addition, during hard times people are short of money but still want to serve, so an increase in servant ministries is also necessary.

The Hard Times Budget Formula
Always Increase:

Worship
Children's Ministry
Evangelism
Marketing
Continuing Education
Volunteer Ministries
Small Groups
Spiritual Formation

CONTINUING EDUCATION

 Changing times require leaders who can change their methods without changing their message, and do it quickly. Historically, the reason most churches have been declining since the 1960s is because from 1960 to 1990 the world fundamentally changed in the way it does everything, but most churches didn't change. In order to effect a change, the leaders needed to be retrained.

But we can hear you saying, "Surely this is an area that can be cut from the budget in hard times." We don't think so. We think it should be increased. Here's why:

During good times people are prone to make drastic, crazy decisions that wind up costing them money over the long term. And why do you think they'd be any different in hard times? Desperate times engender desperate decisions. In hard time, people are prone to make even crazier decisions than before—decisions that can cripple the church.

One of our favorite stories comes from a church we worked with five years ago (this story has been relived thousands of times in different communities over the years). In the late 1980s this declining church sold a large portion of the property it owned to help make it through a downturn in the economy (remember the oil bust in Texas?).

Several years later the economy rebounded; a young, new pastor arrived with a passion for evangelism, and the church outgrew its property. And guess what? The church began negotiating for the purchase of that same property at three times their selling price. Purchasing the adjacent land caused the church to go so deeply in debt it could not afford to build and the growth stopped. Not long after that, the pastor moved on and the church began declining once again. Did they learn anything? Wanna bet there's a "for sale" sign standing in the field?

Now, there are two things wrong with this picture that could have been avoided if the church had not cut the continuing education item from the budget. If the pastor had attended any cutting edge seminar on how to grow a church or the church had spent a few dollars to bring in a consultant, they would have had two revelations. One, don't sell property under the penalty of death. And two, if they had already made the first mistake, they could find a remedy without relocating or repurchasing the property. For instance, they would have known they could lease storefront property down the street at a fraction of the cost of land and building. This would allow them to grow and decide later if they wanted to expand where they were or continue as a multi-site church.

> If you follow our advice, you will avoid making many of the most costly mistakes as you navigate these difficult times.

We are making continuing education easy by offering you three ways to experience inexpensive consultation even in hard times:

- Retrain via the Internet through our online community where hundreds of other Christian leaders are also receiving coaching from us and peer mentoring from one another, as well as through our monthly coaching seminars led by some of the best practitioners to be found. You can find this community at http://church consultations.com/21st-century-strategies/misisonal-church-growth/training/join-the-community/
- Retrain via the Internet, where we provide ongoing coaching based on your particular needs through our Church-Talk radio program (www.churchconsulta tions.com), a variety of webinars, or simply through one-on-one coaching on the phone.
- Engage in a church consultation by mail. You fill out the Complete Ministry Audit and send it to us. We analyze it, send it back to you with recommendations, and then coach you on the phone. This way you can have world-class consultation without the expense of bringing in a consultant. You can find the Ministry Audit by Mail at http://churchconsultations.com/services/mail-consultations/

Of course, nothing quite compares to onsite training and consultations, but the methods listed above each allow you to remain home and save the expense of traveling or bringing in a consultant. In hard times you don't have to forgo the strategic dreaming necessary for your church to thrive.

Remember what we said earlier—hard times require wise decisions by informed leaders. Hard times are not the time to act without all the information you can glean from those who have walked in front of you. So take heart. You're reading this book! If you follow our advice, you will avoid making many of the most costly mistakes as you navigate these difficult times.

VOLUNTEER MINISTRIES

During hard times people lose their jobs. One of the debilitating effects of losing one's job is the loss of self esteem, especially when a family is involved. A person's inability to financially care for the family can be ego-quaking, let alone life-shaking.

One way to bolster a sagging self-esteem is for one to give oneself for the sake of others. Many Christians will want, even *need*, to contribute to the ministry of the church. Without any expendable cash, the only way they can continue supporting the church is by serving as a volunteer. For example, many office positions, such as receptionist, answering the phones, duplication, and other routine tasks can be done by volunteers with minimal training. Helping people keep their dignity by continuing to contribute to the growth of the kingdom is an important face-saving ministry during hard times.

> Many Christians will want, even *need*, to contribute to the ministry of the church. Without any expendable cash, the only way they can continue supporting the church is by serving as a volunteer.

One study done on the effects of the Great Depression found that church attendance actually dropped during the years involved. The reason given was that people could not keep up their appearance and were ashamed to show up at church. We doubt if we are going to see the long lines of people waiting in line for food and clothing that occurred during the Great Depression. But we're already seeing unemployment hit record highs (written in early 2009) and it's likely to only get worse during the next few months. Many of these folks belong to our churches and will deserve a chance to continue to actively participate in a meaningful way. If they are barely able to make ends meet, their contribution won't be money but it can be service.

Such servant ministries accomplish two extremely important things during hard times:

- They allow people to keep some semblance of dignity and continue to support their church and be faithful to their calling.
- They help the church save money on ministries that it might have to drop if it were not for the volunteers replacing paid staff that has to be cut in hard times.

In good times servant ministries are essential, so it should not surprise you we are recommending you increase them during hard times. But we want you to realize they are crucial opportunities for an important segment of your church.

A marvelous website to find thousands of ideas for significant and free servant ministries can be found at Servant Evangelism, http://www.servantevangelism.com.

MOVING ON

One last thought. During hard times anything you can do to combine evangelism and servant ministries will be a big winner. A couple of examples might help here. If you have out-of-work mechanics in the church, offer to fix up cars and charge only for parts. If you have out-of-work carpenters in the church, offer to help people make needed repairs to their homes. If you have out-of-work accountants, offer to help people with their taxes. What other ministries come to mind that might combine evangelism and volunteer ministries for hard times?

Now we move to the last of the Hard Times Budget items— increase small groups and adult spiritual formation.

SUGGESTED READING

Conspiracy of Kindness, by Steve Sjogren. Regal Books (2008), 256 pp.

The Complete Ministry Audit, by Bill Easum. Abingdon (1996), 160 pp.

The Lay Driven Church, by Melvin J. Steinbron. Wipf & Stock (2004), 220 pp.

TEN

BUDGET ITEMS YOU ALWAYS INCREASE IN HARD TIMES

Small Groups and Spiritual Formation

I t's one thing to have all the right ministries in place; it's a far different thing to have the right people leading those ministries. By "right" we mean spiritually mature Christians, not just duty-bound church members. We need spiritual leaders who have proven themselves over the years. By "proven" we mean they have shown both leadership qualities and their humble walk with God. Humbly walking with God doesn't just happen. It takes years of faithfully following God's guidance and searching the Scriptures.

The Hard Times Budget Formula
Always Increase:

Worship
Children's Ministry
Evangelism
Marketing
Continuing Education
Volunteer Ministries
Small Groups
Spiritual Formation

This chapter examines two of the basics of how this maturity happens within the body of Christ.

SMALL GROUPS THAT MEET IN HOMES

Virtually every church professional and scholar today contends that the backbone of adult faith formation is in small groups. Even though small groups are necessary in good times, they are essential in hard times. In hard times people need intimate places to share their hurts and hopes with trusted friends without fear of ridicule. Small groups that meet in homes provide that opportunity.

We are not talking about pure Bible studies but about groups of friends who share life together under the direction of the Scriptures and the Holy Spirit. Nothing can take the place of small groups in good and bad times.

Accountability Question: Do you have someone responsible for the growth and oversight of your small group ministry? If not, this is one of the places to spend whatever money you can. If you don't have the money for a small group champion, find a servant who will do it in their spare time.

We're always surprised, however, at how many church leaders affirm the importance of life-sharing small groups but don't have a viable small group network in their church.

Part of the confusion stems from a misunderstanding of what a small group is. Many church leaders believe that any church group that has less than fifteen or so participants is automatically a "small group." In a way that's true, but in a way it isn't. For instance, a Sunday school class is not a small group—regardless of its size or what you call it. The cornerstone of any effective small group is that there is enough proximity and time spent to build grace-filled, transparent (open and honest) relationships. Small groups are designed to facilitate meaningful relationships more than teach the Bible (although Bible study/discussion can be an integral part of a small group). The bonds of these relationships are nurtured so they can grow deep, and when they do, transparency and encouragement create an atmosphere of camaraderie. When

Christians realize they are in the same boat as one another, fear is replaced with group confidence. That simply doesn't happen in a forty-five minute class on Sunday morning.

Authentic small groups are more life-in-the-faith driven than they are curriculum driven. One of the reasons the majority of *Purpose Driven Life* small groups were unsustainable was that they were curriculum driven. When the Forty Days of Purpose were done, many of the groups were done. They'd completed what church leaders had asked them to do and they didn't understand the disappointed looks in the Christian education pastor's eyes when the groups fell apart.

It's well beyond the scope of this book to do a full training on effective small groups, but here is a bulleted list of the basics. (For a full-blown discussion of small groups, see Bill Easum and John Atkinson, *Go Big with Small Groups*.)

- Don't host small groups on the church campus. The home makes for a more intimate setting as well as an easier place to invite friends. And, we don't need to remind you, it will save the church money.
- Changing and sharing life and the multiplication of the small groups is the primary goal.
- What curriculum you use matters less than the intentional life and faith conversations you have. Use the basic Discipleship Development Questions[1] to guide your agenda. Don't worry if the group doesn't have time to finish (or even start) the scheduled curriculum.
- Everything the "leader" does must be replicable. This means if the leader is expected either to have or to get the answers to questions, you will not be able to replicate them unless you send someone to seminary. So trust the Holy Spirit to help members either recall or deduce answers from the Scriptures themselves. (Keep in mind that all the prevalent and historic heresies came from trained theologians, not laypeople who were honestly searching for answers.)

- Mentor everyone as a leader. Don't presuppose who God can, might, or will use as a future leader.
- Train the group to pray. If someone mentions something that needs prayer, have the group stop whatever they're doing and pray right there. Just-in-time praying is a powerful tool.

> If your leaders aren't living a spirit-filled life before the church, the congregation won't live one either.

- Don't do prayer requests. During the "scheduled" prayer time, the leader should lead and model by opening prayer with three words: "Let us pray" and close the prayer with four words: "In Jesus' name, amen." Expect everyone to lift up whatever prayer needs are on their minds or in their hearts. You can begin the process by encouraging them to either say the name or the need in one or two words, followed by the silent prayer of the group until the next need is lifted up.

Small groups that follow this basic format will discover they grow stronger than any beast that may rear its head in these hard times.

SPIRITUAL FORMATION

Historically, when times get hard, people start turning to the church for hope and assurance. It happened in the 1970s during the recession and the corresponding church growth movement. It happened in the weeks following 9/11. And we're likely to see it again soon. However, if the guests come and discover the church is still business-as-usual, they'll once again return to the darkness from whence they came. The North American church cannot afford to miss this opportunity. So, church leader, you *must* get your spiritual house in order and build a spiritual foundation in your congregation.

We've already addressed your personal spiritual formation in chapter 6. One of the key reasons you *must* deal with your own spiritual development is that without modeling, you cannot build a spiritual foundation within the congregation. One of the axioms of leadership is that leaders actually lead. They go *before* the congregation. When leaders turn around, they see followers. Sadly, in most congregations we discover "leaders" telling the congregation what they should be doing, but the pastor isn't modeling it. Whether the discipline is Bible reflection, prayer, encouragement, or evangelism, if the pastor isn't doing it, the congregation will figure out that it must not be too important. When we find a church that isn't growing and doing adult baptisms and the pastor isn't hanging with the unchurched and sharing his or her faith, we realize immediately that the pastor is leading by example and the congregation is following his or her example to a T.

Modeling is important, but there's more to growing spiritual giants than just being a good example. Mentoring and accountability are also a part of it. We've touched on each of these in earlier chapters, so we'll not dwell on them except to say this. If your lay leadership isn't modeling the spiritual foundations as fervently as the pastor, those who wander into the church during these hard times won't stay. They'll quickly conclude that the church's leadership is as spiritually bankrupt as they are.

It's important that lay leaders in the church be spiritually grounded in good times, but it's critical in hard times. This is not the time to try and activate the uncommitted church member by naming them the chair of some committee. First, it almost never works, but second, this is how churches end up with a board filled with spiritual babies. The primary question to ask before someone is invited into *any* leadership position is "Do they reflect the fruits of the Spirit in every aspect of their life?" (see Galatians 5:22-23). You're not looking for perfection, but you must insist on a "preponderance of the evidence." If they don't, do not make the mistake of putting them into leadership. Remember, if you're going to build a spiritual foundation in your church, it begins with leadership.

Finally, church leaders must be held to a higher standard than those in membership. We recommend that leaders show a significant financial commitment to the church—think tithing—even in these hard times. Leaders should also be expected to be faithful participants in worship *and* in a small group. And it should go without saying that leaders should be expected to show up and lead the ministry they've committed to lead. If they can't live up to these expectations, why would you want them in church leadership?

MOVING ON

That finishes the Hard Times Budget Formula. We hope you will follow our guidelines, because doing so will give you your best chance of coming through hard times a stronger church.

SUGGESTED READING

A Second Resurrection, by Bill Easum. Abingdon (2007), 126 pp.

Go Big! by Bill Easum and Bil Cornelius. Abingdon (2006), 129 pp.

Go Big! with Small Groups, by Bill Easum and John Atkinson. Abingdon (2007), 122 pp.

High-Voltage Spirituality, by Bill Tenny-Brittian. Chalice (2006), 192 pp.

The Apprentice Workbook, by Bill Tenny-Brittian. Booksurge (2007), 174 pp.

Note

1. (1) What did you read in Scripture this week that intrigued you? (2) What is the most significant word/message you heard from God in your listening time this week? (3) How have you shared your faith this week? What was the result? (4) Whose life is different this week because of your witness to Jesus? (5) Who did you encourage in their faith journeys this week?

ELEVEN

LEADERSHIP IN A WILDCARD WORLD

No matter what the circumstances, leadership is always the key ingredient in solving a problem. But when people are undergoing cultural upheavals and catastrophic economic crises, leadership not only becomes more crucial, it also takes some unexpected twists.

> You may be surprised to learn that both the jungle and economic downturns require the same kind of leadership.

This isn't a chapter on leadership in general. It's a chapter on the type of leadership required when the wheels come off and nothing appears to be working. You may be surprised to learn that both the jungle and economic downturns require the same kind of leadership.

The key element of both wildcards is that they are swiftly and constantly changing. Neither stands still. One day the way forward is clear, the next day it is gone. What works well one day doesn't work the next. In other words, what you think you see isn't always what you see. The jungle changes and hard times come on so fast that together they paralyze most people. People stand still while their world falls apart.

Let us ask you. Has your church taken a decisive, proactive response to these two wildcards? Do you still have an annual budget and annual meetings? Do you still nominate leaders on a yearly basis? Have you merely cut your budget and not redirected the money into the "always increase" ministries? If so, you are standing still while the jungle covers you over and the money dries up.

It's time to act proactively. So what kind of leadership do you need in a wildcard world?

QUICK AND DECISIVE

Asking most churches to take quick and decisive action is like asking a turtle to run a marathon. Churches are notorious for taking months to make the simplest decisions. But we're recommending that you throw caution to the wind during these times. Any proactive action is better than none. Instead of "Ready, Aim, Fire," it's "Ready or Not, Fire, then Aim if necessary." We know, this sounds absurd. But these are absurd times that call for absurd action. Remember, if you keep doing what you've been doing, you will keep getting what you've been getting.

Remember my (BE) story in chapter 2 about how we went from three hundred and sixty people making decisions to eleven, with two people having the final say for how money was spent? That's what we mean by quick and decisive. Are you able to do that?

Accountability Question: How long did it take your church to make its last major decision? If it was more than a week, your church is in danger of being left behind in today's crises.

FLEXIBLE

Wildcard worlds are just that—they are wild. They don't play by the normal rules, so they constantly upset our plans. Our plans are often part of the problem in such a world. We spend so much time making the plan, we feel responsible for carrying it out, even if it isn't working.

In a wildcard world leaders must be decisive, but they must also be able to change directions on a dime. On a dime! So throw the plan out the window.

Accountability Question: If your church knows something

isn't working, how easy is it to stop doing it? Are you putting money into a ministry that you have to beg people to attend? Why are you doing that when you now know what the "always increase" ministries are in hard times?

INTUITIVE

In the national park, education was the backbone of society. In a jungle permeated with economic ruin, however, seminary or college do not prepare anyone to lead. All the rules are out the window. What you know is not nearly as important as what you sense about the world around you.

Intuition is the art of sensing what needs to be done without reason. Intuition is an art, not a science. That's why intuition was not a key trait in the national park world. But in the jungle, being able to sense which direction to take is crucial.

> Intuition can't be taught, but it can be nurtured by becoming steeped in the culture.

I'm constantly asking one of my favorite pastors why he does the things he does. One of his most frequent responses is "It just feels like the right thing to do." That's intuition. His actions are based more on his reading of the surrounding community than on anything he learned in college or seminary.

Intuition can't be taught, but it can be nurtured by our becoming steeped in the culture. Both of us have spent huge portions of our lives working in the jungle culture. I (BE) have taken a church through hard economic times (described in chapter 2) and I (BTB) have spent the lion's share of my ministry in the jungle with the unconnected. So we have some gut feelings about what to recommend. The problem is most church people have spent most of their life with national park people, so their intuition isn't much help with the jungle culture.

Intuition is an impossible trait when people are scared and tired. That's why great leaders always know they must take care of their spiritual and physical needs before they can help others. If this is true in normal times, it is imperative in hard times.

Accountability Question: Are you spiritually and physically healthy enough to be able to intuit what needs to be done to proactively address these hard times? If not, then turn the leadership reins over to someone else and let them lead. Then you go out and spend some time in the jungle.

SELF-REGULATED

The actions of leaders determine the spiritual climate of a church. If the leaders overreact to crises by becoming paralyzed, it filters through the congregation. If the leaders appear to be frightened, the congregation will become frightened. If the leaders lose their cool, the congregation will begin to come apart.

We recommend the leaders never show fear or disunity or indecision in front of the congregation. Instead, describe the reality and the seriousness of the situation—and in the same breath share how the church is going to proactively respond to the crisis.

Accountability Question: How do your leaders handle pressure? Do they keep their cool or do they wring their hands?

LET THE YOUNG LEAD

If you are over the age of thirty-five and resonate in your gut (intuition) with what you've read, then lead. If on the other hand, you don't resonate with our recommendations, it may be because of your age or how you grew up. You probably were born into the national park world. There's nothing wrong with that—both of us were born into that world. But we've seen more of the Christian landscape than most people, and we feel in our gut that what we've written is on track. If you do too, then lead. If not, we recommend you turn over the leadership of the church to some younger leaders who can stomach our recommendations because they were born into the jungle and aren't afraid of it.

Leaders under the age of thirty-five are more apt to have the above traits than most people our age. We know. Just saying this sends most church leaders into spasms because the average age of most people in established churches is now over sixty. But it's true. Mature leaders, if you feel overwhelmed with what is happening in today's world, why not give some of your promising younger leaders a chance to lead? You might be surprised at how well they deal with the emerging world.

MOVING ON

By now you either have a clear picture of how to lead or you have decided we're crazy. We hope it's the former because we really want to help your church navigate through these hard times. We firmly believe in what we have recommended in these pages. There's only one more thing we need to share with you.

SUGGESTED READING

Leadership on the Other Side, by Bill Easum. Abingdon (2000), 217 pp.

Practicing Greatness, by Reggie McNeal. Jossey-Bass (2006), 192 pp.

TWELVE

IT'S A WASTE OF TIME IF . . .

E verything we've said so far is true. It's not true for just
select churches. It's not true for just big churches or just
small churches. It's universally true for all churches in
hard times. Of course, all we've said up until now could be a
total waste of your time and ours if . . .

YOUR CONGREGATION TOLERATES UNRESOLVED CONFLICT

When guests show up to your worship service, they've overcome nearly insurmountable obstacles to be there. They've
entered foreign territory and they've made it into your presence. Their spiritual discernment antennae are up and on high
alert. They're not just checking out your hospitality; they're
checking out your authenticity, your integrity, and your relationships. If there's unresolved conflict between your members, you can be sure their hypersensitive sensors will pick it
up and warning alarms will sound.

You may think we're being overdramatic, but time after
time we find unresolved conflict literally killing a church. If
you have ongoing conflict, you can make a heroic attempt at
everything we've said in this book and it will be for naught.

Resolving conflict isn't pleasant. The majority of church
leaders we coach and consult with are honest enough to admit
that they hate dealing with conflict. Rather than dealing with
it directly, though, far too many pastors and leaders make

excuses for the bad behavior of the few and secretly hope if they just ignore it long enough it will go away. Here's a late-breaking news flash: it won't. Conflict that is unresolved clouds the congregational climate worse than fog covers the Thames.

The Solution

There has been a lot written about conflict management over the years, but we're here to tell you that conflict *management* is not the Christian response. Jesus was pretty clear that we're not to manage conflict—we're to resolve it. He gave the church specific instructions about conflict resolution and Matthew captured his instructions.

Step One: Model and embed Jesus' conflict command in Matthew 5:23-24.

- "So when you are offering your gift at the altar, if you remember that your brother or sister has something against you, leave your gift there before the altar and go; first be reconciled to your brother or sister, and then come and offer your gift" (Matthew 5:23-24).

  Notice that the onus in on *you*, the practicing disciple of Jesus, to take the first step of resolving the conflict. If you know you've caused offense, whether real or perceived, it's incumbent upon you to make the first move. Teach this in your congregation. Embed it. Insist on it. Model it. Live it.

Step Two: Rely on Matthew 18:15-17 when someone misbehaves.[1]

- "If another member of the church sins against you, go and point out the fault when the two of you are alone. If the member listens to you, you have regained that one" (Matthew 18:15).

  After an incident, the pastor or board chair immediately visits the controller one-on-one and says, "As a congregation, we've agreed that we will not treat one another like this. Your behavior wasn't in keeping with our expected behaviors. This cannot continue." If an apology and repentance is offered, the issue is done. If, on the other hand, the controller refuses to repent or makes excuses or turns the blame on the board/pastor/committee/church, or someone else, conflict resolution goes to the next level.

- "But if you are not listened to, take one or two others along with you, so that every word may be confirmed by the evidence of two or three witnesses"(Matthew 18:16).

The pastor or board chair reports to the executive committee (if the board is over twelve people). Then two people, the original visitor and one other (typically an elder or a senior member of the board/executive committee) goes to the controller and says essentially the same thing as in the first visit, except this time they are told that the behavior will not be tolerated and that it must cease. If there is repentance, the issue is done. If not, the conflict resolution goes to the final level.

- "If the member refuses to listen to them, tell it to the church; and if the offender refuses to listen even to the church, let such a one be to you as a Gentile and a tax-collector" (Matthew 18:17).

The two visitors next report to the board (the whole group this time) about the visits. The board should discuss the issue and the behavior. If the board agrees that the behavior is inconsistent with the congregation's expected behaviors, they have no choice but to invite the controller to appear before them. If the controllers come (highly unlikely in our experience), the board informs them that their behavior is unacceptable and if the behavior does not immediately cease, the board has no choice but to remove the controllers from all leadership positions and to instruct them to not return to the church until he or she has decided to behave otherwise. In other words, show the controllers the door and tell them to not come back until they've had a change of heart. If that change of heart should break forth, the controllers must first seek reconciliation with the pastor and then the board.

Conflict Resolution Isn't Easy

Is this process easy? No. We've had to use it several times during our ministry. It's painful and hurtful and unpleasant. But in every case—and we mean *every* case—when the offending person is removed, there is a collective sigh of relief by the congregation. Attendance goes up (after the supporters of the controller leave in protest), giving goes up, and the spirit of the church improves significantly. Another side benefit is that other would-be controllers take notice, and when they act out (and they will), you'll seldom have to get past the one-on-one confrontation. They know the congregation is not afraid to be faithful to Jesus and his conflict instructions.

Of course, we can hear someone saying, "But that's not a nice thing to do." We agree, asking someone to leave the church isn't a nice thing to do, but it is biblical. God's mission through the church is too important to allow a handful of people to hold it hostage. For more on this, see our article "On Not Being Nice for the Sake of the Gospel."[2]

Fail to resolve conflict in your church and you waste your time trying to effectively grow your church.

DON'T MISS THE OPPORTUNITIES GOD GIVES YOU

Put it all together and it comes down to this. As a congregation you've been given the task to follow Jesus, the North Star of the church, into the real world to make disciples. If your congregation continually blows the opportunities God sends you, why would God risk sending you any more?

Congregations that are embroiled in conflict, that lack a rock-solid spiritual foundation, that tolerate mediocrity, that are unwilling to make changes in their own traditions to communicate the gospel effectively to the unconnected are on the road to destruction. There's hardly room for churches like these in good times. There's absolutely no room for them in hard times.

Church leaders simply *must* take the lead in these times and effect church transformation. If that's not possible, take Jesus' instructions seriously when he told his followers, "If they don't receive you, kick the dust off of your sandals as a testimony against them" (Matthew 10:14). We can't afford to waste good leaders on unresponsive and unregenerate churches. Go find a place of peace where God can send you opportunities to change lives and invite your networks to have a firsthand experience with God.

MOVING ON

Now you know what you have to do to effectively minister in hard times. Is there anything keeping you from doing it? Not unless you allow it. So take charge.

SUGGESTED READING

Antagonists in the Church, by Kenneth Haugk. Augsburg (1988), 192 pp.

Friedman's Fables, by Edwin H. Friedman. The Guilford Press (1990), 213 pp.

Notes

1. Misbehavior is almost always the result of someone trying to control decisions for his or her own benefit. These controllers must be reined in or the ministry of the church will be hamstrung.

2. For one of our most asked-for articles over the years ("On Not Being Nice for the Sake of the Gospel") go to http://easumbandy.com/the_community/community_resources/articles/articles_by_bill_easum/on_not_being_nice_for_the_sake_of_the_gospel/

APPENDIX

WORSHIP LEADER JOB DESCRIPTION

Position Objective
To provide pastoral leadership to the worship ministries based on the mission or vision statement of your church.

Position Description
The worship leader is responsible for every aspect and detail of each worship service, including the spiritual guidance of everyone in the music ministry and any special events. This person pulls together the teams that make worship happen.

Qualifications
1. A growing relationship with Jesus Christ and an ability to effectively communicate it
2. Impeccable character
3. Commitment to the mission, vision, and worship philosophy of your church
4. Demonstrated credentials, i.e., has shown the ability to grow teams for worship

Abilities
1. This person does not have to be ordained.
2. A heart for shepherding those in the music ministry
3. Relates well with people
4. Skilled in the use of all aspects of worship technology
5. Ability to use other art forms as needed
6. A team player with a positive attitude

Responsibilities
1. Build the necessary teams to carry out the worship areas of (your church)

2. Plan the corporate worship services of the church, in consultation with the senior pastor
3. Serve as lead worshiper in all worship services
4. Direct all weekly rehearsals necessary to facilitate worship in services
5. Provide pastoral care for the worship teams and choirs
6. Oversee the worship department budget, organization, and volunteers
7. Set annual goals for the worship ministry that are in line with the church's vision and then evaluate how those goals were attained or modified during the year